# Who's Who of British Beheadings

# Who's Who
## of
# British Beheadings

*Geoffrey Abbott*

Yeoman Warder (ret'd) HM Tower of London
Member of Her Majesty's Bodyguard of the
Yeoman of the Guard Extraordinary

André Deutsch

First published in 2000 by
André Deutsch Ltd
76 Dean Street
London W1V 5HA
www.vci.co.uk

Reprinted 2000

A catalogue record for this book is available from the
British Library

ISBN 0 233 99774 1

Typeset by
Derek Doyle & Associates, Liverpool.
Printed and bound in the UK by
Mackays of Chatham plc, Chatham, Kent

Back jacket photograph by Jeremy N McCabe
Line drawings by Jil Atkinson
Photographic work by Ed Geldard, Photo Workshop,
Kendal, Cumbria

This book is dedicated to all those who clung to their firm beliefs and despite the odds against them yielded not their principles but lost the battle and their heads.

# CONTENTS

# ACKNOWLEDGMENTS

# ACKNOWLEDGEMENTS

To Brian Harrison, erstwhile Yeoman Warder, Honorary Archivist of the Tower of London and Freeman of the City of London for his definitive compilation of all known prisoners held in the Tower of London; Dr Harold Hillman, Reader in Physiology and Director of Unity Laboratory of Applied Neurobiology at the University of Surrey for his advice on the anatomical effects of decapitation; to the staff of the National Museum of Antiquities of Scotland in Edinburgh, and to the many librarians and curators who patiently sifted through their shelves and archives in order to satisfy my insatiable desire for little known and fascinating facts!

Whilst every effort has been made to trace copyright to material in this book, the author apologises if he has inadvertently failed to credit any ownership of copyright.

# INTRODUCTION

From the days of the Normans in the eleventh century until the mid-1900s, capital punishment was meted out in various ways, by hanging, burning, beheading or being hanged, drawn, beheaded and quartered.

Decapitation, the subject of this book, was the penalty inflicted for relatively serious crimes against the sovereign, the individual, the state or its religion. It was adopted as a judicial punishment by William the Conqueror, one of the first to be so dispatched being Waltheof, Saxon Earl of Huntingdon, in 1076 Simon, Lord Lovat was the last, in 1747.

Execution by the sword was, with few exceptions, super-seded by the heading axe; in the sixteenth and seventeenth centuries Yorkshire and Scotland also employed guillotine-type machines to perform the task, the former possessing the Halifax Gibbet, the latter employing the Scottish Maiden. In the abhorrent penalty of being hanged, drawn and quartered, the head was removed by the 'ripping knife' after it had been used to disembowel the victim.

Many of those decapitated had been found guilty of committing high treason, a large number being of noble or aristocratic birth and so by virtue of their rank eligible for imprisonment in a royal fortress, the Tower of London, rather than in a gaol for common criminals. Because their crime had threatened the security of the state, the state prison, the Tower, was the most appropriate place for their incarceration.

Over the centuries thousands were found guilty by the courts and beheaded; these pages feature one hundred of those unfortunates, a selection spanning a broad cross-section of society, detailing each by name and background, their crime, sentence and the disposal of their remains.

# METHODS OF EXECUTION

# THE HEADING AXE AND BLOCK

Being dispatched by cold steel rather than being hanged was granted as a privilege to those of royal or aristocratic birth, it being considered less ignoble to lose one's life as if slain in battle, rather than being suspended by the hempen rope. Such privilege, however, did not necessarily make death any less painful; on the contrary, although being hanged brought a slow death by strangulation, the axe was little more than a crude unbalanced chopper. The target i.e. the nape of the neck, was small; the wielder, cynosure of ten thousand or more eyes, nervous and clumsy. And, even when delivered accurately, it killed not by cutting but by brutally cleaving its way through flesh and bone, muscle and sinew. It was, after all, a weapon for punishment, not for mercy. Women were rarely dispatched by this means, but were sentenced to death by being burned at the stake, with the added concession, sometimes but not always, of being strangled before the flames mounted.

Most executions by the axe took place in London, the weapon being held ready for use in the Tower of London. The one currently on display is believed to be that which severed the heads of the three Scottish lords who led the Jacobite Rebellion in 1745, Lords Balmerino, Kilmarnock and Lovat. It measures nearly thirty-six inches in length and weighs almost eight pounds. The blade itself is rough and unpolished, the cutting edge ten and a half inches long. Its size and the fact that most of its weight is at the back of the blade means that when brought down rapidly, as of course it would be, the weapon would tend to twist slightly, throwing it off aim, and so it would fail to strike the centre of the nape of the victim's neck. Unlike hangings, executions by decapitation were comparatively rare events, the executioner thereby being deprived of the necessary practice. A further factor was that the axe's impact inevitably caused the block to bounce. If therefore, the first stroke was inaccurate and so jolted the victim into a slightly different position, the executioner would need to readjust his point of aim for the next stroke – no mean task while being subjected to a hail of jeers, abuse and assorted missiles from the mob surrounding the scaffold. It was probably a combination of these factors which resulted in James, Duke of Monmouth receiving no fewer than five strokes before complete decapitation was achieved. One likes to think that the first stroke rendered the victim unconscious, but who knows?

The Heading Axe should not be confused with the fifteenth-century Ceremonial Axe, also held in the Tower of London, which is carried on ceremonial occasions by the Yeoman Gaoler. This has a blade twenty inches long and ten inches wide, its wooden shaft being five feet four inches long, adorned with four rows of burnished brass nails along its length. In the days before radio and television, this symbolic weapon was used to indicate to the crowds lining London's streets the verdict passed by the court on the latest celebrity prisoner. The condemned man or woman was, of course, escorted by Yeoman Warders of the Tower and accompanied by the Yeoman Gaoler who, by carrying the Axe with its edge pointing towards the prisoner, indicated that the verdict was one of Guilty; on but few occasions did it point away, signifying Not Guilty. This practice could well have been the forerunner of that tradition-ally employed to indicate the verdict in a naval court martial; the accused, on returning to the room following the court's deliberations, is immediately apprised of the verdict by the position in which the sword on the members' table is pointing; if at the accused, the verdict is Guilty, and vice versa.

The Heading Axe's vital partner, the Block, was a large piece of wood of rectangular section, its top sculptured specifically for its gruesome purpose. Because it was essential that the victim's throat rested on a hard surface, the top had a hollow scooped out of the edges of each of the widest sides; at one side the hollow was wide, permitting the victim to push his – or her – shoulders as far forward as possible, the hollow on the opposite side being narrower to accommodate the chin. This positioned the victim's throat exactly where it was required, resting on the flat area between the two hollows. Blocks were usually about two feet high so that the victim could kneel, although the one provided for the execution of Charles I was a mere ten inches in height, requiring him to lie almost prone and thus inducing in him an even greater feeling of total helplessness.

## THE EXECUTION SWORD

Rarely used for judicial executions in England, the most notable being that of Queen Anne Boleyn, the sword was employed in Scotland until the middle of the sixteenth century, records showing that in 1552 ten shillings (50p) was paid 'for the sharping of the commone Sweird ilk tyme it was usit', and in February 1563, 'The Baillies and Councall ordaines Mr Robert Glen the Treasurer to coften fra William Makeartnay his two handed sword to be used for ane heiding sword, because the auld Sword is failzet, and to give him five pounds thairfor.' It was also recorded that in that year, 'twa men were condemnid to be heided with ane sword.'

This type of weapon was widely used on the Continent for

dispatching those condemned to death; had it been adopted in England, much unimaginable suffering by the victims of the axe could have been avoided for, in contrast, the execution sword was a finely honed and superbly balanced instrument of death. About three feet or more in length, it weighed approximately four pounds; the two-inch-wide blade had parallel cutting edges and a broad, blunt tip, no point being necessary to achieve its purpose. A wide groove, or 'fuller', ran longitudinally along each side to allow the blood to flow towards the handle and not coagulate and so blunt the razor-sharp edges. The comparatively long handle, designed to be gripped with both hands, was covered with leather or fish-skin to provide a non-slip surface, the quillons, the guards, being wide and straight.

Contrary to popular belief, the victim did not kneel over a block. Had he or she done so, the headsman himself would also have had to kneel and deliver a vertical blow, which would, inevitably have lacked the force necessary to decapitate his victim. And if, instead of kneeling, the executioner had stood erect, the blade would have struck the further edge of the block rather than the victim's neck. The procedure, therefore, was for the victim to kneel upright or to stand, the executioner swinging the blade horizontally round his head once or twice to gain the necessary momentum before delivering the fatal stroke. If undue suffering and horrific flesh-wounds were to be avoided, 'co-operation' by the victim was essential, for if he or she swayed or trembled too violently, more than one blow would be required.

## HANGED, DRAWN AND QUARTERED

To conspire against the sovereign, the very personification of the nation, was considered equivalent to plotting the downfall of the country and so the charge was one of high trea-

son, the gravest offence known to the law (low, or 'petit treason', a term rarely used, was the crime committed by a wife in
murdering her husband, or a servant his master i.e. for killing,
not the ruler of the country, but the 'ruler' of the household).
High treason called for the direst punishment possible, more
severe even than being hanged or beheaded, and those guilty
of such a heinous crime would stand in the dock and hear the
judge utter the sentence, the dread words of which varied but
slightly over the centuries:

> The court doth award that thou shalt be had from hence
> to the place from whence thou did come, and so drawn
> through the open city of London upon a hurdle to the
> place of execution, and there to be hanged and let down
> alive, and thy privy parts cut off and thy entrails taken
> out and burnt in thy sight; then thy head to be cut off, and
> thy body to be divided into four parts, and to be disposed
> of at the Sovereign's pleasure; and may God have mercy
> on thy soul. (*Suspendantur et viventes ad terram poster-
> nantur, et interiora sua extra ventes suos capiantur
> ipsiusque viventibus comburantur*).

The phrase 'hanged and let down alive' was, of course, so that
the victim would not be spared the sight and agony while the
remainder of the sentence was being administered. The
method of hanging in those days never brought about a rapid
death anyway. The rough hempen rope with its primitive slip
knot, together with a short drop of only three or four feet,
meant a slow, lingering death by strangulation. This practice
remained unaltered until the nineteenth century, when the
executioner Marwood introduced the merciful 'long drop'
method in which the distance the victim had to fall – usually
between six and ten feet – depended on his or her weight, build
and general fitness, death coming almost instantly by the

dislocation of the neck's vertebrae and severance of the spinal cord.

The probable sensations induced by a 'short drop' hanging were best described by the executioner William Calcraft who, after dispatching a condemned man at Lancaster Castle, was asked what it must have felt like to the victim. His reply, quoted in a guidebook of 1893, was: 'Well, I have heard it said that when you are strapped up and your face turned to the Castle wall and the trap falls, you see its stones expanding and contracting violently, and a similar expansion and contraction seems to take place in your own head and breast. Then there is a rush of fire and an earthquake; your eyeballs spring out of their sockets; the Castle shoots up in the air and you tumble down a precipice.' As good an assessment as anyone can get, from one in the trade. And if sentenced to be hanged, drawn and quartered, then, at some stage of that appalling ordeal, the victim would be cut down and the brutal castration would start.

The intent of that particular operation was to prevent the accused from producing any offspring as traitorous as he – a purely symbolic act, since the victim was put to death anyway. Then the heart – 'from whence cometh the treacherous thoughts!' – together with the bowels and other organs would be 'drawn', that is, removed by the 'ripping knife' and thrown on the fire burning by the scaffold. Not until then would the head be severed and the body hacked into four pieces, all being taken away in a basket to be parboiled in a cauldron containing salt water and cumin seed in order to deter the birds from eating the flesh of the 'exhibits' for as long as possible. John Newman, a convict who was imprisoned in Newgate in 1670, described in his autobiography the room in the gaol known as 'Jack Ketch's Kitchen':

a little place like a closet neer where we lodged, and in it lay the quartered bodies of three men who had been executed some days before. Their quarters had lain there so long because their relatives were still seeking permission to bury them which at length with much ado was granted. But only for the quarters, not for the heads, which were ordered to be set up in some part of the City. I saw the heads when they were brought up to be boiled; the hangman brought them in a dirty dust basket, out of some place, and setting them down among the felons, he and they made sport of them. They took them by the hair, flouting, jeering and laughing at them; and then giving them ill names, boxed them on the ears and cheeks. When done, Jack Ketch [the name of a particularly brutal hangman subsequently applied to his successors] put them into his kettle and parboiled them with Bay-salt and Cummin-seed . . . the whole night was both frightful and loathsome and begat an abhorrence in my nature.

The sentence of being hanged, drawn and quartered was never passed on women found guilty of high or petit treason. The historian Blackstone stated that the possible reason for this was in deference to the sensitivity of public feeling: 'As the delicacy due to the sex forbids the exposing and public mangling of their bodies, their sentence – which is to the full as terrible to sensation as the other – is, to be drawn to the scaffold and there to be burnt alive.'

Men sentenced to be hanged, drawn and quartered were usually dragged on hurdles to London's Tyburn, the Ty-bourn being a small stream which once flowed there. The area was originally called 'The Elms', after the trees which bordered it (the elm was considered by the Normans to be the tree of justice), and was situated by the main road leading into the capital from the northwest. The spectacle of the scaffold, with the corpses of those who had merely been hanged swaying on the gibbets was obviously intended to have the greatest deterrent effect on visitors to the city. The precise site of the earlier executions is difficult to determine since the gallows, known as the Tyburn Tree, ceased to be a permanent structure from 1759, after which they were taken down after use and reassembled whenever required. However, there is little doubt that the scaffold itself stood near the junction of Edgware Road and Oxford Street (the latter once named 'Tyburn Way'). In fact, should one venture on to the small traffic island there, a plaque will be found, set in the cobbles, bearing the words 'Here stood Tyburn Tree. Removed 1759'. But in view of the fast-moving traffic, extreme caution should be exercised lest yet another tombstone should bear the inscription 'Died at Tyburn'! (For more information, see also p.189.)

## HEADS ON LONDON BRIDGE

After the half-strangling of those unfortunates sentenced to be hanged, drawn and quartered, followed by evisceration and dismembering, their quarters were displayed on the gates of those cities in which they had resided and plotted, London, Newcastle, Carlisle, York, Shrewsbury and the like. However, most of the heads, together with those of traitors decapitated by the axe, were exhibited in the capital, spiked on London Bridge, where they remained for months until thrown into the River Thames by the bridge watchman, usually to make room for new arrivals. The bridge was chosen as the most appropriate venue because, for over six centuries, it was the only river-crossing in London, forming a continuation of Watling Street, the Roman road which traversed Kent from the Channel coast. As at Tyburn, the grisly exhibits were visible warnings to all entering the city from that direction, of the awful retribution meted out to those who sought to overthrow the realm. On the bridge a visitor would find himself approaching a gateway against which the drawbridge immediately in front of it had, for three centuries, been winched up when attack threatened or to allow tall-masted ships to pass through. A parapeted gallery ran across the top of the arch and, on raising his eyes, the visitor would see, leaning at all angles, a dozen or more pikes, their number depending on the results of recent treason trials, the majority being adorned with a human head, although here and there a gory quarter would intrude.

Foreign visitors occasionally remarked on the sights that confronted them as they rode over the bridge. Jacob Rathgeb, the Duke of Wurtemberg's secretary, reported seeing 'about thirty-four heads of persons of distinction who had in former times been condemned and beheaded for creating riots'. Another foreigner, Joseph Justus Scaliger, visiting the capital in 1566, observed: 'In London there ever were many heads on the bridge; I have seen there, as if they were masts of ships and at the top of them, quarters of men's corpses.' Thirty or so years later, in 1602, the Duke of Stettin warned his compatriots of the autocratic powers of the Tudors. 'For near the end of the Bridge, on the suburb side, were stuck up the heads of thirty gentlemen of high standing who had been beheaded on account of treason and secret practices against the Queen.' Some gory remains actually adorned the Tower itself, a contemporary describing that edifice as: 'the grim fortress from whose battlements, as from the towers of the Bridge which faced it, hung the bodies of scores of traitors drying in the sun. The heads of many another grinned at the passers-by from the pikes upright along the tops of the walls, food for the carrion birds that fought for their possession till only a whitened glistening skull remained.'

Within the Tower was located the Royal Mint, charged with the manufacture of the nation's coinage, and in about 1560 the task of melting down and refining the metal of large numbers of base coins was carried out by Germans brought to London by an alderman named Lodge. Due to the noxious fumes given off during this process, probably due to the arsenic with which the metal was mixed, many of the men became seriously ill and, mindful of a superstition current at the time, they were advised that they would be cured by drinking from the skull of a dead man. Accordingly, the worthy alderman and those in charge of the Mint obtained a Warrant from the Council 'to take of the headds uppon London Bridge and made cuppes thereof, whereof they [the Germans] dranke and founde some relief althoughe the mooste of them dyed.'

From about 1678 the venue was moved, heads and body segments being displayed within the city itself. Although today Westminster is taken to be just another part of London, it was not always so; originally both were separate cities, one demarcation line between them being an archway named Temple Bar positioned approximately at the juncture of the Strand and Fleet Street. The original wooden gate was destroyed in the Great Fire of 1666 and was replaced in 1672 by an elegant structure built of Portland stone designed by Sir Christopher Wren at a cost of £1397 10s. 0d. The royal coat of arms was emblazoned above the central arch but the stone heads of the four statues which adorned the edifice, those of Charles I and II, James I and Elizabeth I, were soon joined by the human ones from the Bridge, the prominent position of the archway on such a busy thoroughfare guaranteeing maximum publicity and, it was hoped, deterrence.

By 1790 however, the general public were campaigning to have Temple Bar removed, various pressure groups having their own reasons: some claiming that it provided cover behind which pickpockets lurked, others, that it impeded ventilation and was downright ugly. In 1877 it was decided that the structure proved such a hindrance to building development and had become such a bottleneck to the rapidly increasing amount of horse-drawn traffic, that it was dismantled and banished to Theobald's Park, Hertfordshire. Although reportedly in a ruinous condition, it was listed as an historic building in 1954 and as an ancient monument nine years later. It is hoped that current plans to have it rescued and reassembled somewhere in London come to fruition – for purely historic and decorative purposes, of course.

## THE HALIFAX GIBBET

This beheading machine was not actually a gibbet (a frame on which bodies of those who had been hanged were displayed as deterrents), neither was it a gallows, but a guillotine-type instrument, albeit in existence centuries before the French model was introduced in 1792. That any method of execution should still be in local use centuries after private and feudal methods of execution had been abolished was itself an anachronism, but in the sixteenth and seventeenth centuries Yorkshire was to a great extent a kingdom in its own right. It was bounded by the sea to the east and the Pennine hills to the west; almost impenetrable forests lay to the north and, until the Dutchman Sir Cornelius Vermuyden introduced a land drainage system, wide-spreading fens covered the regions to the south.

The construction of the Halifax Gibbet was described by Holinshed in his *Chronicles* published in 1587:

The engine wherewith the execution is done, is a square block of wood of the length of four and a half feet, which doth ride up and down in a slot, rabet or regall, between two pieces of timber that are framed and set upright, of five yards in height. In the nether end of the sliding block is an axe (blade), keyed and fastened with an iron into the

13

wood of the block which, being drawn up to the top of the frame, is there fastened by a wooden pin, unto the middest of which is a long rope fastened.

The identity of the inventor is lost in the mists of time but, according to *The Pinder of Wakefield*, published in London in 1652: 'A Fryer lived there in those dayes that was very ingenious, he invented an Engin, which by the pulling out of a pin, would fall and so cut off the necke, this device kept them in awe a great while till at the last this Fryer had committed a notorious fact, and for the same was the first that hanseled the new Engin his own invention.' In other words, he got it in the neck!

The authority governing the use of the machine was the Halifax Gibbet Law which stated that any felon caught with stolen goods either hand-habend (carried in the hand) or back-berand (carried on his back) or confessed to stealing goods to the value of thirteen pence halfpenny (6p) or more – by the Common Law of England, death was the penalty for the theft of goods to the value of twelve pence, giving the accused leeway of three halfpence – would be put on trial before a jury of sixteen local residents. Other than the town bailiff, no judge or lawyer was present, the jurors were not under oath, and no appeal was permitted. The only actual officer of the law involved was the coroner, and his services were not required until after the execution.

If found guilty on a Saturday, the day on which the widely attended cloth market was held, that being the local industry, the condemned man or woman would then be taken direct to the gibbet and beheaded. Otherwise they would be held in the town gaol and secured in the stocks during the two markets held on other week days, with the stolen goods displayed alongside them, and executed on the following Saturday.

The operation was quite straightforward and on the face of

it, totally democratic, for no officially appointed executioner was employed; instead, the long rope holding the securing pin was stretched out into the crowd and, if they agreed that the prisoner deserved to die, they pulled the rope, the pin fell out, the block ran down the grooves in the uprights and the blade, seven pounds twelve ounces in weight and measuring ten and a half inches in length and nine inches wide, severed the kneeling victim's head. Those spectators too far away from the rope to pull it, would signify their concurrence by stretching their arms in the direction of the rope. And should the miscreant have stolen an ox, sheep, kine or similar animal, the rope would instead be tied to its halter, the bailiff would whip up the beast – and poetic justice would truly be done.

That the machine's action was effective was endorsed by Holinshed: 'The block wherein the axe is fastened, doth fall with such a violence that even if the neck of the transgressor be as thick as a bull, [the head] would still be cut asunder and roll from the body by a huge distance.'

The Halifax Gibbet, situated appropriately on Gibbet Hill and approached via Gibbet Street and Gibbet Lane, was reportedly in action as early as 1286, although not until 1541 does the town's register record any names, the first of the total of fifty-three since that date being Richard Bentley of Sowerby. The instrument was dismantled in 1641 but, probably due to an increase in the local crime-wave, was reassembled in 1645, the last men to position their necks between its uprights being Wilkinson and Mitchel in 1650 (see p.223 for a description of their misdemeanours). However, its use was finally forbidden by Oliver Cromwell in 1650, the town's criminals being subsequently executed by the national facilities situated at Tyburn and elsewhere.

By 1738 only the five-foot-high base and the steps leading up to it remained, overgrown with grass and weeds, and James Cooke, writing on 12 January 1814, lamented the fact that some of its outer supporting walls of sandstone had been removed by local residents on which to site their newly acquired ovens. Totally obscured from view by rubbish, the base was eventually excavated in 1839 and a stone tablet with the inscription 'Halifax and its Gibbet Law' erected on the site. Since the 1970s, much excellent restoration has taken place and the blade itself is displayed in the Museum situated in Halifax's historic Piece Hall.

# SCOTTISH MAIDEN

It is traditionally believed that James Douglas, Earl of Morton, Regent of Scotland, while returning home following a visit to the English court, passed through Halifax, Yorkshire, and in doing so, saw the Halifax Gibbet. Whether an execution was actually taking place is not known, but suffice it to say that so impressed was the earl that on arriving in Edinburgh he ordered a similar machine to be constructed. It became known as the Scottish Maiden (Madin or Maydin), a name perhaps derived from the Celtic mod-dun, the place where justice was administered.

Made of oak, the Maiden consisted of a five-foot-long horizontal beam to which were fixed two ten-foot-long posts, mounted vertically, these being four inches wide by three and a half inches thick, bevelled at their corners. These were sited twelve inches apart and braced by two further lengths of timber attached to the horizontal beam, being secured to the uprights at a height of four feet from the ground. A further brace at the rear held the machine in the upright position, it being attached to a cross rail which joined the two posts together. The axe blade was an iron plate faced with steel, thirteen inches in length and ten and a half inches in breadth, its upper side weighted with a seventy-five-pound block of lead.

The blade travelled in copper-lined grooves cut in the inner surfaces of the posts and was retained at the top by a peg attached to a long cord which, when pulled by means of a lever, allowed the blade to descend at ever-increasing speed.

Three and a quarter feet from the ground, a further cross-bar joined the two posts, serving as a support for the victim's neck. This beam, eight inches broad and four and a half inches thick, had a wide groove cut in its upper surface filled with lead to resist the impact of the falling blade after it had passed through the flesh, muscle and spinal column. To prevent the victim withdrawing his or her head, an iron bar, hinged to one upright, was lowered and secured to the other upright before the peg was withdrawn and sentence carried out.

In contrast to the Halifax Gibbet, it was operated, not by the burghers of the city, but by the official executioner, the 'Lokman', who was also responsible for its serviceability, it being recorded, for instance, that in 1660 'Alexander Davidson is to mainteane it all the dayis of his life.' The city accounts reveal a variety of payments: in 1582 sixpence was paid to the Lokman for drinks with which to quench his thirst and two shillings and eightpence 'for twa poks of bran [sawdust] to spread about the Maiden'. Even more macabre, in 1600, twelve shillings and eightpence was spent 'for ane barrell to salt the quarteris with salt thareto', while thirty shillings and fourpence was forthcoming 'to the lokman for the executing and putting up [on display] of the heidis and quarteris'.

Despite its name it showed no favours to women, its blade descending on Isabell and Ann Erskine in 1614 for poisoning their two nephews, Marion Astein for adultery in 1631 and Janet Embrie who was found guilty in 1643 of committing incest with two brothers. Nor did the Maiden hesitate for a moment three years later when required to decapitate Margaret Thomson, wife of the minister of Balmaclelland, for adultery, Christian Hamilton in 1679 for murdering Lord

17

Forrester in Corstorphine, or Marion Maxwell who, in 1694, together with Daniel Nicolson, committed adultery and forgery; she was beheaded, he was hanged.

All executions took place in public, the machine usually being positioned near the City Cross in Edinburgh's High Street, although it could be transported by cart to other cities as required. Many Scottish heads fell beneath its blade between 1564 and 1710, when its use was discontinued. The machine (blade raised in readiness) is now on display in the superbly appointed National Museum of Antiquities of Scotland in Edinburgh.

## THE EXECUTIONER

In the days when life was short and disease was rife, when existence for the lower classes was a daily struggle to survive and humane consideration for the wrong-doers, as prescribed by the law, was minimal, death on the scaffold, however violent, was accepted by the populace as the norm, and to many, as a regular source of entertainment. Little or no consideration was given to the possible suffering of the victim, for had not he or she attempted to remove or replace the monarch, or to change the country's religion, or committed some hideous crime? So why hone the axe razor-sharp? Why go to all the trouble of training a man to aim it accurately and mercifully? Why allow the victim to die on the rope before disembowelling him with the ripping knife? After all, the victims were there to be punished – and punished they were. Deterrence was the name of the game and as a negative cannot be proven, the question as to whether it worked remains unanswered. The legal responsibility for the execution of criminals, by whatever means, was that of the Sheriff, the word derived from 'shire-reeve', he being the chief officer of the Crown of each county or shire. That official, however, in order to avoid having to do the distasteful job personally, 'sub-contracted' it out to anyone who volunteered and so the task of beheading, or of hanging, drawing and quartering the condemned person, was undertaken by the hangman, the title describing his more usual occupation.

Those who tightened the noose, swung the axe or wielded the ripping knife were men of their times, most of them lacking sensitivity or imagination, many of them brutal and callous. Since they were employed only when the occasion demanded rather than as civil servants, few if any records were kept of their names; anonymity was also essential to avoid retribution being wreaked by the supporters of those they had executed. Paid in part by their victims in the futile hope of a speedy and merciful demise, loathed and abused by the public at large, they nevertheless provided services that were, however repugnant to modern society, essential. Without them all those engaged in administering the law of the land, the judges and lawyers, the court officials and the juries, would have been totally redundant.

## POSSIBLE DURATION OF CONSCIOUSNESS

Modern medical opinion is that the brain is irreversibly damaged if the blood ceases to flow through it for five minutes, but what happens before that time has elapsed? It has been conjectured by some eminent pathologists and neuro-biologists that when the head is severed by a sword or a rapidly falling 'guillotine-type' blade, there is sufficient oxygen remaining in the brain to prolong consciousness for perhaps two, three or even more seconds after decapitation. Dogs are conscious for up to twelve seconds after the blood supply to the brain has ceased and it is a proven fact that after a person or

animal has been killed, organs surgically removed for trans-
plant purposes continue to function, hearts to beat, kidneys to
produce urine. So, if these organs are not dead, is a severed
head? And if the head is still living, is the 'owner' still
conscious? If so, could the victim see the ground or basket
coming up to meet him or her – even perhaps have sufficient
time to witness the gloating faces of those clustered round the
scaffold as the head is brandished by the executioner? It was
reported that when Anne Boleyn's head was held high, the
eyes and the lips continued to move. Just muscular reaction?
Or the last vestiges of consciousness? Alas, like death itself,
only those who personally experience decapitation can know
what happens – and within what time-scale.

# CASE HISTORIES

## ARROWSMITH, Father EDMUND

Despite the appalling likelihood of being decapitated and brutally disembowelled, their bodies then hacked into several pieces and displayed on city gates, there were nevertheless, men so dedicated to their religious principles, so unswerving in their faith, that even such a hideous fate could not deter them from pursuing their holy calling. Many faced that possibility and, regrettably, many paid that unimaginable penalty. Father Edmund Arrowsmith was just such a man.

He was born in 1585 to Robert Arrowsmith, a yeoman, and his wife Margery, at Haydock in Lancashire, and was christened Bryan or Barnaby. Always a pious and delicate child, he was described as being small and somewhat uncouth, though of a bright and pleasant disposition towards his fellows. At the age of twenty he went to Douay College, the religious centre of exiled Roman Catholics in northern France, where his uncle was a professor, and there, on receiving the Sacrament of Confirmation, he adopted the name Edmund. Accepting that his destiny was to become a priest, he studied hard and eventually, on 9 December 1612, he achieved his ambition and returned to England to administer to those who were being persecuted by the authorities because their religious beliefs were contrary to those of the Protestant Church.

For ten years he travelled on horseback throughout his home county, narrowly avoiding arrest on many occasions; although once confined in Lancaster Castle he was later released and continued his mission to bring solace to those who needed his

spiritual support. But the blow fell in 1628 when he was visiting a friend, Mr Holden, who lived in the Blue Anchor Inn in
the locality of Brindle. The tavern, a half-timbered house, was
periodically used by the priest as a place of refuge, containing
as it did a secret priest hole entered via one of the bedrooms
beneath its thatched roof. But it failed to provide sanctuary on
this occasion and the disaster which overtook him can only be
attributed to his strict adherence to the sanctity of marriage.

It so happened that two first cousins of the Holden family
living at the inn had recently been married by a Protestant
minister. The groom was a Catholic, his bride a Protestant,
although she intended to change her religion to that of her
husband, and so had sought Father Arrowsmith's help in
procuring the necessary dispensation to validate the marriage.
When the document arrived from Rome, the priest insisted
that it could not be implemented until the couple had
remained apart for the qualifying period of fourteen days.
Incensed at the delay, the couple took the unbelievably vindic-
tive action of betraying their mentor. Knowing when he would
be arriving, they informed Captain Rawsthorn, the local
Justice of the Peace, but that gentleman, being a friend of Mr
Holden, warned the innkeeper in advance of the action he
would have to take. Accordingly, Father Arrowsmith quickly
mounted his horse and rode away, only to be intercepted by the
Justice's servant, and as the man was armed with a sword, he
had no alternative but to submit to capture.

A local legend circulating shortly afterwards related how a
farmer named Crook, who had volunteered information to the
pursuers as to the route taken by their prey, was later
rewarded with the priest's cloak and had a suit made out of it
for his young son who, on first wearing it, went for a ride on
his favourite horse. But on this occasion the animal, hitherto
quite tractable, reared up and threw the boy off, with fatal
results. The legend also averred that the children of later

generations of that family were born stunted, one of them, a dwarf named James, alias 'Turk', being drowned in the River Darwin in February 1862.

Taken to Lancaster Castle, Father Arrowsmith was imprisoned in the dungeons. On 28 August 1628 he was placed on trial, found guilty and sentenced to be hanged, drawn and quartered. He was led to where the gallows had been erected, about a quarter of a mile from the castle. There the cauldron bubbled over the fire burning near the scaffold and the vast crowd waited impatiently. The official hangman, a local butcher, refused to perform the grisly deed and the execution was eventually carried out by an army deserter under sentence of death in the gaol for absconding from his regiment. The reward he demanded was forty shillings, his freedom and the prisoner's clothes.

Father Arrowsmith mounted the ladder which had been propped against the cross-beam, the noose was placed round his neck and the rope pulled taut. The renegade soldier then twisted the ladder, throwing his victim off, and within minutes had cut down the half-strangled priest and the hideous procedure commenced. The martyr's last and dying words were '*Bone Jesu!*' as the ripping knife did its work. His severed quarters were later displayed over the massive portal of Lancaster Castle known as John of Gaunt's Tower.

Not all his remains were so abused, however, for one of the warders at the castle, Henry Holmes, rescued some of the body parts and sent them to another priest, later writing a letter of authentication in which he said:

The certainty of those things which I did deliver you at your being at Lancaster, I will affirm to be true, for the hair and the pieces of the ribs I did take myself, at the going up of the plumbers to see the leads [on the battlements], when they were to mend them; and the handkerchief was dipped in his blood at the time of his quarters coming back from the execution to the Castle, by me likewise with my own hands. You know the handkerchief was your own which you gave to me at your departure, and for the piece of the quarter, both I and some others had taken part of it for our friends, and that which I gave to you, the chief warder John Rigmaden, gave me leave to take.

Nor were those the only relics, for a local family of devout Catholics acquired not only the knife used in the disembowelling, but the martyr's right hand which, according to Dom Bede Camm in his book *Forgotten Shrines*, published in 1910, was later preserved to the memory of Father Arrowsmith in St Oswald's Church in Ashton, wrapped in linen and enclosed in a silver casket, since when many miraculous cures were attributed to its holy powers.

## ASKE, ROBERT

Defying Henry VIII always led to serious trouble, often fatal, but some people never learned, and Robert Aske was one of that unfortunate category. At that time, in 1536, English society was in a state of turmoil. Among other things, taxes and prices were rising, northern wool merchants were opposing new regulations instituted in their industry and calls for a freely elected parliament at York went unheeded. But probably the main grievance concerned the dissolution and destruction of the monasteries which had been ordered by the King in order to destroy the feudal power of the abbots and confiscate their wealth for the benefit of the royal coffers. But many of these northern places of worship were neither rich nor endowed with valuable icons; on the contrary, they were part of the fabric of their local communities, the monks working with the peasants, administering not only spiritual aid but, where needed, food and medicine. Demolition of their monasteries deprived them of shelter, the lead from the roof, the very stones of the walls being taken to build houses for the more prosperous citizens. Finally, popular outrage came to a head and the mass protest which became known as the Pilgrimage of Grace erupted, thousands taking to the road in an attempt to register their grievances and obtain justice. The marchers declared their intention to free the Court of evil counsellors such as the Lord Chamberlain (Thomas Cromwell) and the Duke of Norfolk, and to restore the religious institutions. The pilgrims fastened scrolls on their breasts displaying the five wounds of Christ, each group marching behind the cross of its church. One large assembly happened to encounter a hunting party near Appleby in Cumberland, a member of which was Robert Aske. He was a lawyer from the East Riding of Yorkshire, an astute man with the charisma and ability to inspire the crowds of illiterate peasants, a man who was doubtless greedy for the power which the protest marchers offered if he would lead them. Accordingly he consented and set about organizing the campaign, with the result that similar rebellions sprang up across Cumberland, Yorkshire and other northern counties. Although Aske was in charge of what was nothing more than an undisciplined horde of 40,000 pilgrims, nevertheless, under the threat it posed, the city of York surrendered, as did Hull and Pontefract Castle. In the following months, Lord Darcy of Pomfret Castle, Sir John Bulmer from Norham Castle, together with Thomas Percy, brother of the Earl of Northumberland, and other of the landed gentry all joined the Pilgrimage.

At the increasing prospect of serious civil disobedience, the alarm bells sounded in London and the Duke of Norfolk entered the political fray. In order to play for time, he met Aske and some of the other leaders, promising a full pardon and a free Parliament. At a secret meeting with Lord Darcy he attempted to split the opposition, saying, 'I advise you to take, dead or alive, but alive if possible, that arrant traitor Aske, which will extinct the ill bruit and raise you in favour of his Highness.' Honest Darcy, however, refused to double-cross his leader, and at the seeming victory they had achieved, many of the protesters felt satisfied and returned home.

Having not the slightest intention of surrendering to the commoners, Henry suggested that Aske should come to the Court 'with diligence and no man privy thereto'. When Aske approached Darcy for his advice, the noble lord urged him to go, adding, 'And if he holds you I will rescue you from the Tower!' At the meeting the King reassured Aske that York would indeed get its parliament, and removed any of Aske's final doubts by giving him a gift of a jacket made of crimson satin.

But by the following year, when it became apparent that the King had reneged on his promises, that no parliament would be established at York and that garrisons of soldiers were to be stationed in Newcastle, Hull and Scarborough, another violent resurgence broke out. The lawyer's character was summed up by the historian Hall, who described him as 'a man of base parentage yet of marvellous stomach and boldness; he had shown great ability in commanding the rebels on the first breaking out of the insurrection but had received the King's pardon. He was soon afterwards sent for to court and taken into favour, but there lived not a verier wretch as well as in person as condition and deeds, and as soon as the insurrection began again, he absconded and once more put himself at the head of the rebels.'

Henry VIII, determined to stamp out this challenge to his supreme authority, sent Norfolk to crush the latest violent outbreak, demanding that monks participating in the march be imprisoned and that those women who had cut down the bodies of their hanged husbands, dug their graves and buried them themselves at night, be severely punished. Norfolk did not hesitate to obey his master's orders. Courts were set up, their packed juries condemning hundreds to death. The small fry swung from the gallows or worse, the *Grey Friars Chronicle* recording: 'On this yere 1537 the xxv day of Marche the Lyncolnechere men was browte owte of Newgate vn-to the yelde-hall [Guildhall] in roppys, and there had their jugment to be drawne, hongyd and heddyd, and qwarterd, and soo was the xxix of Marche after, the wyche was on Maundy Thursdaye, and alle their qwarters with their heddes was burryd at Pardone churche-yerde in the frary.' A martial law at Carlisle sentenced seventy-four pilgrims to be hanged and the leaders themselves knelt over the block, Lords Darcy, Percy, Bulmer and other knights mounting the scaffold steps on Tower Hill. Of their fellow aristocrats, Lord Hussey was beheaded at Lincoln and Sir Robert Constable hanged in chains at Hull. Lord Bulmer's wife, who took an active part in the Pilgrimage, was burned to death at the stake at London's Smithfield.

In May 1537 Robert Aske was also brought to the Tower and persuaded to reveal every detail of the Pilgrimage and name all those involved. He accepted the blame and, realizing the fate which had overtaken him, pleaded that his family be spared. He put his affairs into order, asking that his belongings, including the King's gift, be collected from the Cardinal's Hat tavern in the City and brought to the Tower. And finally, fearful for the manner of his own end, begged, 'Let me be dead ere I be dismembered.' It is doubtful whether his plea for a merciful dispatch was granted, the records simply showing that he was taken under heavy guard back to York and, on Thursday 28 June of that year, he was hanged, then beheaded, his remains festooning the gates of that city as a warning to all.

# BARKSTEAD, SIR JOHN

A man who with others had signed King Charles I's death warrant, who had buried treasure in the Tower of London and whose head finally adorned Traitors' Gate in that royal castle, can hardly be classed as having had an uneventful life, though no doubt there were times when he wished he had never deserted his earlier profession as a goldsmith in the Strand. But desert it he did, to join Oliver Cromwell's forces as a captain in the Roundhead army during the Civil War. So impressed was the Great Protector with the captain's leadership qualities that not only was Barkstead chosen to be one of those who sat in judgement on Charles I, he was also appointed Governor of Reading and later became Member of Parliament for Colchester.

Further honours followed for, on 12 August 1652, Cromwell awarded him the post of Lieutenant of the Tower of London. Our hero, always with an eye to personal gain, realized that rich pickings were to be made at the Tower, most of its prisoners being Royalists who could afford, and were prepared to pay, exorbitant sums of money for luxury meals to be sent in from outside catering establishments (the more upper-class taverns on Tower Hill), and for the privilege of being allowed to walk along the battlements, under escort of course, for fresh air, exercise and a view over the city. There was no doubt that the Lieutenant was good at his job, the essayist and historian Thomas Carlyle quoting Cromwell's comments that 'there was never any design on foot but that we could hear about it out of the Tower. He who commanded there would give us account that within a fortnight or so there would be some stirring.'

His star was definitely in its zenith, for not only did he become Major-General of London (pay-scale £2000 per annum) but in 1656 was appointed to the lucrative post of Steward of the Protector's Household and made a knight as a mark of Cromwell's appreciation. By the year 1659 he had become a very rich man, having amassed a veritable fortune believed to be in the region of £50,000, but word of the acquisition of such large sums of money reached the authorities and he found himself summoned to appear before the investigatory Committee of Grievances. Fearing, not unnaturally, that his ill-gotten gains would be confiscated, he packed most of his riches, consisting of gold coins, in butter firkins (small barrels) and reportedly buried them in a cellar somewhere in or near the house he occupied in the Tower, the Lieutenant's Lodgings (now the 'Queen's House').

As he had anticipated, the Committee not only severely censured him but dismissed him from his post and, being denied the opportunity to retrieve the treasure he had buried he retired, chastened, to his estate in Acton, Middlesex. Any hopes of ever digging up his precious firkins faded even further when, less than a year later, popular opinion finally turned against the Commonwealth and Charles II was invited to reign over the country instead. Fearing that retribution would be levied against those officers who had condemned his father to death, as indeed it was, many of the regicides wasted no time in fleeing to the Continent, Sir John taking up residence in Hanau, Germany. There he became a burgess, an accepted citizen of that town, but nostalgia proved too much for him and in 1661 he decided that it would be safe, if not to return to England, at least to have a reunion with a couple of fellow regicides, Colonel Okey and Miles Corbet, in Delft, just across the border in the United Provinces, Holland. But just as they were discussing old times in an ale-house in the Hooft Straet 'over a Pot of Beer and a Pipe of Tobacco', they were arrested and handed over to the English Resident.

That gentleman, at best a turncoat, at worst a traitor, had been a republican but on seeing which way the wind blew, hastily changed sides and, declaring himself a born-again Royalist, inveigled his way into the diplomatic service and was sent to Holland as the King's representative. His name was George Downing, and it is to be hoped that his unsavoury character is not being repeated by those occupying the London street named after him! Without a moment's hesitation he had his three captives – under one of whom, Colonel Okey, he had served in the Civil War – sent back under guard to England in the ship *Blackamore* and, ironically for Barkstead, imprisoned in the very castle which he had commanded.

All those who had signed the death warrant of Charles I at his trial had themselves already been found guilty of high treason and condemned to death *in absentia*, and it only required positive identification of the trio at the King's Bench court on 16 April 1662 to confirm that sentence. Accordingly, three days later they were taken in the cart to Tyburn and there hanged, drawn and quartered. Colonel Okey showed much penitence and in consideration of his valour and otherwise good character, his friends were allowed to claim his severed quarters and give them a decent burial in hallowed ground. No such concession, however, was allowed in respect of his two comrades in arms, their quarters being exhibited over the City's gates. And while Corbet's head was spiked on London Bridge, that particular part of the late Sir John Barkstead's anatomy returned to his previous residence, being skewered on a pole above Traitors' Gate in the Tower of London. But its lolling tongue kept its secret, for although many have sought to find the gold-packed firkins, including Samuel Pepys, no one is known to have discovered the Lieutenant's loot.

For a full account of the famous diarist's search and the possible location of the treasure trove, I refer potential treasure hunters to my book *Mysteries of the Tower of London*, published by Hendon, 1998, but would remind them that taking metal detectors and mechanical diggers into that royal palace is strictly forbidden.

# BARLOW, FATHER EDWARD AMBROSE

Father Barlow was a Jesuit priest during the reign of Charles I, a dangerous time for Catholics, for although the Queen was a member of that Church, the King yielded to Parliament's demands that Catholic priests should be hunted down and persecuted, a proclamation eventually being issued to the effect that all priests failing to leave the kingdom within one month would be classed as traitors and so suffer accordingly. Despite the pleadings of his supporters, Father Barlow refused to consider deserting his flock, or even to go into hiding – a decision with disastrous results, for at Easter 1641, while the Jesuit was celebrating Mass at Morleys Hall in Lancashire, not far away the Reverend James Gatley was ministering to his Anglican congregation at Leigh Parish Church. The vicar, a man of fiery zeal, lost little time in inflaming the tempers of his listeners against the Papist who was preaching the idolatrous Mass up at the Hall and, without much difficulty, exhorted them to attack and capture the priest. Over four hundred parishioners, armed with clubs and swords and led by the vicar clad in his surplice, marched to the Hall and surrounded it, breaking down the doors and rounding up those who had been worshipping at the altar. Father Barlow surrendered to the mob, his flock being released after they had given their names and addresses, and been warned of future judicial action to be taken against them.

Following his appearance before a Justice of the Peace named Risley, the prisoner, escorted by sixty armed men, was taken to Lancaster Castle and there imprisoned. Four months later, on 7 September, he was brought to trial. There was little prospect of any mercy being shown; the Judge, Sir Robert Heath, having received instructions from Parliament to impose the extreme penalty upon any priest convicted at Lancaster, 'for a terror to the Catholics who were numerous in that county'. After a short trial, he was found guilty and sentence was passed, decreeing that he should be hanged, dismembered, quartered and boiled in tar.

On 10 September 1641 he was drawn on a hurdle from the castle's gateway to the nearby place of execution and suffered the fate imposed on traitors. So great was the crowd surrounding the scaffold that the executioner had considerable difficulty in carrying out the various gory stages of the execution. It was hardly surprising therefore, that in the mêlée, some of the priest's devout followers among the spectators managed to rescue the martyr's left hand and part of one of the fingers of the right hand, together with a piece of bone. The hand was given to the Benedictine nuns of Stanbrook Abbey, Worcester as a holy relic, 'the skin being like old parchment, the thumb and index finger pressed together and the little finger pressing against the ring finger; the nails almond shaped, broken and uneven'. Other portions, a piece of rib and a metacarpal bone were also rescued and presented to various abbeys and convents.

After severance, the head was impaled on a pike and displayed, it is believed, on the tower of Manchester's Collegiate Church, now the Cathedral. It was rescued from there by one Francis Downes who lived about five miles from the place of Father Barlow's capture, in Wardley Hall, an historic house in which the priest had often conducted surreptitious services.

Over a century later, in 1745, during the restoration of a ruined part of the building, an old chest was discovered which, when broken open with a pickaxe, was found to contain a skull, complete with almost a full set of teeth and still retaining plenty of auburn hair. Unfortunately, a maidservant, in tidying the room later, found the skull and, thinking it to be a hunting trophy, threw it into the moat. That night a storm raged which was of such magnitude that the superstitious owner of the Hall, Matthew Moreton, attributed it to the indignity heaped on the skull. Accordingly he had the moat drained and retrieved the grim relic. Subsequent research having identified it as that of Father Barlow, the head remained at Wardley Hall, a mute testimony to the persecuted martyr.

Understandably over the next two hundred years, legends sprang up regarding the skull and its reportedly supernatural powers; disturbing it would result in strange and violent sounds in the night, treating it with disrespect would cause windows to be shattered, cattle to die, inhabitants to contract rashes and diseases. In the early years of this century the skull was believed still to be in Wardley Hall, securely ensconced in a glazed niche set within an inner wall of the main hall so that it was visible from both sides, though screened by oak doors when necessary to protect it from those who would scoff at such a holy relic.

## BARTON, ELIZABETH

Born about 1506, by the age of nineteen Elizabeth Barton was employed as a maidservant in Aldington, Kent and after contracting an epileptic-type disease, became subject to trances. The visions she experienced while in this state seemed real to her and she gained the reputation of having second sight. This alleged ability was cunningly manipulated into religious channels by local monks, the news of such a 'Divine Gift' being widely publicized, even eventually reaching the ears of Sir Thomas More and Bishop William Fisher of Rochester who, it was reported, arranged for her admittance to the Benedictine Nunnery of St Sepulchre at Canterbury in 1527.

Elizabeth, by then known as the 'Holy Maid of Kent', was so

incensed by the divorce brought by Henry VIII against Catherine of Aragon that, convinced by the intensity of her religious fervour, she preached vehemently against the King, prophesying that he would die a villain's death within a month of marrying Anne Boleyn. Neurotic ramblings could be ignored – high treason could not. Thus in June 1533 she was taken to the Tower and put to the torture, then carried in procession to St Paul's Cross to perform public penance. That minor punishment was, however, considered far from adequate and such was the Catholic support for her beliefs that in January 1534 she was condemned to death. On 20 April of that year she was taken to Tyburn and there hanged. It is not known whether she was cut down only half-strangled, as was usual in such cases, or whether some time elapsed before she was finally decapitated by the axe. Her head was later spiked on the Drawbridge Gate of London Bridge, the only woman to be so exhibited, 'its long black locks falling over its pallid features as a terrible warning to all'.

## BLOUNT, SIR THOMAS

This knight, Deputy Naperer to Richard II in 1377 (i.e. an *ex officio* post nominally in charge of the royal linen) was one of the King's loyal supporters and when Richard abdicated in September 1399 in favour of Henry, son of John of Gaunt, Sir Thomas joined a conspiracy led by the Earl of Kent and the Earl of Salisbury to overthrow the new King. The plan was to surprise Henry IV at a tournament to be held at Windsor in December of that year, but one of the conspirators, the Earl of Rutland, leaked the plan to the King, who promptly raised a strong force of troops in London and set out for the rebels' headquarters in Windsor. The conspirators fled to Cirencester but were rounded up and more than thirty of them were executed, some being 'drawen, hanged and beheded at

Tyborne'. Most, however, were taken under strong guard to Oxford, among them being Sir Thomas Blount, whose suffering was surely the most horrendous ever recorded. 'Sir Thomas Blount was hanged,' wrote a witness to the scene,

> but the halter was soon cut and he was made to sit on a bench before a great fire; and the executioner came with a razor in his hand and knelt before Sir Thomas, whose hands were tied, begging him to pardon his death, as he must do his office. Sir Thomas asked, 'Are you the person appointed to deliver me from this world?' The executioner answered, 'Yes, sir. I pray you pardon me.' And Sir Thomas kissed him and pardoned him his death.
>
> The executioner knelt down and opened his belly and cut his bowels straight from below the stomach and tied them with a string that the wind of the heart should not escape, and threw the bowels into the fire. Then with Sir Thomas sitting before the fire, his belly open and his bowels burning before him, Sir Thomas Erpyngham, the King's Chamberlain, came and, insulting Blount, said in derision, 'Go seek a master now that can cure you!' Blount only answered, '*Te Deum Laudamus*! Blessed be the day on which I was born, and blessed be this day, for I shall die in the service of my Sovereign Lord, the noble King Richard!' The executioner knelt down before him, kissed him in a humble manner, and soon after, his head was cut off and he was quartered.

## BOLEYN, QUEEN ANNE

Anne Boleyn was described by Giustinian, the Venetian Ambassador as being 'not one of the handsomest women in the world, of middling stature, swarthy complexion, long neck, wide mouth, bosom not much raised, her eyes black and beautiful, her hair the colour of a raven's wing'. Others commented even more adversely on the strawberry-sized mole on her throat – known as the devil's paw-print – and the right-hand little finger being split so that it looked double, both obvious signs of a sorceress. Some went so far as to revile her by calling her a 'goggle-eyed whore', even encouraging the court idiot to chant 'Anne is a ribald and her child is a bastard.' Nevertheless she was young, she was attractive, she was flirtatious – and so, eventually, she was beheaded.

Whether that ghastly fate could have been avoided had she given Henry VIII the healthy son he so desperately wanted in order to maintain the royal lineage, or had Henry responded to her alleged affairs simply by divorcing her and banishing her from the kingdom, is open to conjecture. But her downfall was really foreshadowed in January 1536 when, after the birth to a still-born boy, it became unlikely that she would ever have any more children. Once over her grief, however, she continued to flirt with the young courtiers around her, unaware that the malicious gossip circulating about the court, especially the intense dislike directed at her by Lady Rochford, wife of her brother George, had reached Henry's ears.

That the Queen was totally unprepared for the disaster which was about to overtake her is evidenced by two inventories held among State Papers. As late as 28 April – only four days before her arrest – Anne ordered some red fringe to enhance the harness of the horses that pulled her coach, and paid for 'a cap of taffeta, covered with a caul of damask gold for the baby Princess Elizabeth and other rich materials'. Among a list of loans was one of £100 to her attendant Lady Worcester, a lady treacherous enough to betray some of her secrets to Henry VIII. Shortly after the Queen's execution, Lady Worcester wrote to Thomas Cromwell, the King's right-hand man, begging him to cancel the debt 'in such a manner that her husband, Lord Worcester, should never know anything about it, as she dreaded the consequence of the revelation.'

It was on Mayday, at a tournament held at Greenwich, that the simmering situation finally erupted. Anne dropped a kerchief which was picked up by Henry Norris, Groom of the Stole; King Henry, apparently furious, immediately rose and returned to London, taking Norris with him. En route, he accused the young man of committing adultery with the Queen, hinting at a pardon if a confession was forthcoming. Norris, shocked, denied any impropriety, but despite that, was arrested and taken to the Tower of London. On 2 May Anne herself was accused of 'evil behaviour' by her uncle the Duke of Norfolk and taken into custody by Sir William Kingston, Constable of the Tower. Distraught, not even having had time to change out of the magnificent robe of crimson velvet and cloth of gold which she had worn at dinner, she was escorted under Traitors' Gate and asked tremulously, 'Am I to go into a dungeon?' The officer reassured her, saying that she would occupy the rooms in which she had spent the night before her coronation. All pleas to be allowed to see her daughter Elizabeth were refused, and further disturbing news came when she learned that her brother George, together with those alleged to have consorted with her, namely William Brereton, Sir Francis Weston, Henry Norris and her favourite spinet player, Mark Smeaton, had all been arrested. Nor was that all, for her arch-enemy, Jane Rochford, had an audience with the King during which he closely questioned her, that unscrupulous lady doubtless seizing the opportunity to blacken further the Queen's character.

Anne was accused of committing adultery and treason and after a lengthy trial in which, among other charges, it was testified that only a month after giving birth to Elizabeth, she was unfaithful with Norris, with Brereton on 16 November, with Norris again on 19 November and Brereton again on 8 December 1533 – and finally to have committed incest with her brother George in Christmas week.

She was found guilty, the Duke of Norfolk declaring, 'Because thou hast offended our Sovereign the King's Grace in committing treason against his person, and here attainted of the same, the law of the realm is this; that thou shalt be burnt here within the Tower of London, on this Green, else to have thy head smitten off as the King's pleasure shall be further known of the same', the only concession being that His Majesty granted her the unique privilege of being decapitated by the sword rather than the traditional axe.

Three days before her execution, Anne was visited by Archbishop Cranmer who brought a document for her to sign which annulled her marriage to Henry VIII on the grounds of a pre-contract (engagement) she had had to marry Henry Percy, Earl of Northumberland. Reportedly Anne denied the agreement and also swore she had always been faithful to the King. Henry Percy had attended her trial and, overcome by the stress of the proceedings, tragically had a fit and died a year later.

In the Tower Anne was closely guarded. Not only was she denied the company of her personal gentlewomen, but her two minders, her cousin Lady Boleyn and the ominously named Mistress Coffin, had strict orders to report everything she said and did. Nor was that all, for the Constable and his wife slept outside her door on an improvised bed.

By the eve of her execution her moods not unnaturally became mercurial, verging on hysteria. She said to Sir William, 'I hear that I shall not die before noon and I am very sorry therefore. For I thought to be dead now, and past my pain.' Seeking to reassure her, he replied that there would be no pain, to which she replied, laughing heartily, 'I have heard the executioner is very good, and I have a little neck!'

On 19 May she arose at 2 am and had three Masses and Holy Communion, then ate a little breakfast at 7 am before returning to her room for more prayers. At 11 am Sir William opened her door and conducted her to where the grim cortège was waiting, led by two hundred Yeomen of the Guard, the escort being followed by the executioner, who had been brought over specially from Calais (which was still an English possession at that time). He was dressed, as tradition demanded, in a black tight-fitting suit, a half-mask covering the upper part of his face, with a high, horn-shaped cap on his head. This grim uniform, new for the occasion, had been paid for by the Constable of the Tower, Record Office accounts showing that the officer had received one hundred crowns in French currency, about £23 in English currency, 'to give to the executioner of Calays for his rewards and apparail'. Next came the Tower officers, noblemen of the Court, the Lord Mayor and aldermen of the City of London, followed by Anne herself, dressed in a loose robe of black damask over a red under-skirt. She wore a deep white collar, furred with ermine, her rich, black hair hidden by a small hat, under which was a white coif. In one hand she carried a white handkerchief, in the other a little prayer book bound in gold. Many of those present described how attractive she looked, her cheeks flushed, and her eyes, although red with weeping, shining unusually brightly.

On Tower Green all was ready, the Constable having ordered his deputies to 'send for Master Eretage for carpenters to make a scaffold of such height that all present may see it'. Accordingly it stood five feet high, surrounded by a low rail and, of course, strewn with straw. Anne took her leave of her companions and gave the prayer book to one of them, after which she allowed herself to be assisted up the steps by Sir William. Looking around at the gathered assembly, she declared in a clear and calm voice that she was innocent of the dreadful charges brought against her, swearing that she had always been a true wife to the King. Those nearest to the scaffold described her final audible words: 'Mother of God! Pray for me. Lord Jesus! Receive my soul.' Her cape was removed and she took off both black cap and coif, replacing them with a white linen cap. She then knelt, as did most of the spectators (no block was used when the execution was by the sword) and when their prayers had ended, Mistress Lee, her lady-in-waiting, bound her eyes with a linen handkerchief. After which, according to an eyewitness, 'she prepared to receive the stroke of death with resolution, so sedately as to cover her feet with her nether garments'.

The executioner, who had considerately concealed his sword under the straw, then signalled to his English assistant to approach the Queen, the sound thereby distracting her attention, and as she turned her head slightly, he seized his opportunity; grasping the weapon, he swung and, with a single blow, severed her head. Instantly blood gushed copiously over the boards of the scaffold, and several women were seen to faint as the headsman lifted the head on high, gasps of horror coming from the onlookers as the eyes and lips were seen to open and close convulsively.

The historian Crispin, in an account written two weeks after her death, described how: 'her ladies immediately took up her head and the body. They were so languid and weak with anguish, but fearing that their mistress might be handled unworthily by inhuman men, they forced themselves to do this duty and at last carried off her dead body wrapt in a white covering.'

Although the executioner was otherwise well organized, no arrangements had been made to provide a coffin and so a Yeoman Warder had to obtain a wooden arrow-chest from the nearby armoury, into which the head and body were placed. It was carried into the Chapel Royal of St Peter ad Vincula within the Tower. However, as it was then, reportedly, too late in the day for the customary Mass to be said, Father Thirlwall, her personal chaplain, pronounced a blessing over the rude coffin before it was deposited in a vault under the altar, close to that which contained the mangled remains of her brother Viscount Boleyn who, together with Brereton, Norris and Weston, had been beheaded in public on Tower Hill two days before.

During the reign of her daughter Elizabeth, the vault was described by an anonymous visitor:

The coffin of the Duke of Northumberland rests besides that of the Duke of Somerset, between the coffins of the Queens Anne Boleyn and Katherine Howard, and next unto these last is the coffin of Lady Jane Grey. Then comes the coffins of Thomas Seymour, Lord of Sudeley, and of the Lady Rochford; and lastly that of George Boleyn, that was brother to Queen Anne – all beheaded!

In 1876, by command of Queen Victoria, the exhumation and possible identification of these remains and others took place. Excavations beneath the altar revealed the coffins of all the Tudor victims still in their places, though extremely dilapidated and in most instances merely heaps of dust and pieces of wood intermingled with bones, whole or in fragments. Among them were the remains of a young female having 'a well-formed round skull, intellectual forehead, straight orbital ridge, large eyes and a square full chin,' as described by Mr Doyne Bell, one of the committee members present. From these characteristics and the small vertebra discovered – evidence of Anne's 'little neck' – the remains were identified by Mr Mouat, a surgical expert, as being 'all consistent with public descriptions of Queen Anne Boleyn, and the bones of the skull might well belong to the person portrayed in Holbein's painting of the Queen.'

These remains, together with those of the others buried there, were reverently reinterred, being individually placed in thick leaden coffins. Their covers were soldered down and they were then deposited in boxes of oak plank one inch thick, the lids of which were secured with copper screws. To each box was attached a leaden escutcheon with the name of the person supposedly enclosed, and all were buried four inches below the surface of the altar. The whole area was then concreted over and overlaid with green, red and white mosaic marble, the designs having borders of yellow sienna marble and bearing the names and crests of some of the victims.

For many decades, on each anniversary of Anne's execution, bunches of roses have been delivered to the Tower with an anonymous request that they be laid on her tombstone. The Yeoman Warders on duty there comply with this request, conscious of the fact that, although they are sworn in at St James's Palace as Members of the Queen's Bodyguard of the Yeomen of the Guard Extraordinary, their predecessors were regrettably unable to prevent the tragedy which took place within the Tower on that particular date so many centuries ago.

## BOLEYN, GEORGE, VISCOUNT ROCHFORD

To become a viscount as well as a member of the royal family, many people would be prepared to pay an arm and a leg, but where George Boleyn was concerned, it cost him a part of his anatomy that he could ill afford to lose – his head! The son of Sir Thomas Boleyn, Earl of Wiltshire, he was created Baron Boleyn of Rochford in about 1530, and on 25 January 1533 became brother-in-law to the King, that being the day on which his sister Anne married Henry VIII. After that, honours flowed, among which were the appointments as Constable of Dover Castle and Lord Warden of the Cinque Ports.

Some four years before receiving his knighthood he had married Jane Parker, daughter of Henry, first Lord Morley, and for some unknown reason, whatever affection had first attracted her to her husband soon turned to hate, and hate him she did. Nor was this aversion restricted to George, for her intense loathing extended to his sister Anne, to whom she was a Lady of the Bedchamber. Lady Rochford's feelings of hatred were given full rein when the scandal involving Anne and her alleged love affairs reached the ears of the King, for it was believed by many that she was responsible for the charge later brought against her husband, that of committing incest with his sister. The only evidence of such a serious offence was flimsy indeed, relying as it did solely on the fact that one morning he had entered Anne's bedroom before she was up and, in speaking to her, in the presence of her maids, had rested his hand on the bed. Incest was serious enough, but incest with a queen was automatically high treason and so both charges were brought against the unfortunate man. Nor was that all: witnesses testified that he had abused the King by contemptuously criticizing the monarch's dress and ballads and, infinitely worse where Henry was concerned, by saying, 'that the King was not able to have relations with his wife; that he had no virtue or potency in him'.

George Boleyn was sent to the Tower of London on 2 May 1536 and there, thirteen days later, was brought to trial immediately after his sister had faced her judges. No prosecution witnesses were produced and an acquittal seemed possible, it being reported that Rochford 'replied so well that several of those present wagered ten to one that the charges would be dismissed'. But the jury that day consisted of twenty-six peers of the realm and they, having just found his sister guilty, wasted little time in passing the same verdict, the sentence being that he too, be beheaded.

On 17 May, two days before the execution of his sister Anne, he and three others found guilty of intimacy with the Queen, were decapitated by the axe in public on Tower Hill where, it was said, 'the executioner shed tears, but the bleeding corpses were allowed to lie on the scaffold for hours, half-dressed'. Eventually, his remains were carried back into the castle and buried beneath the altar of the Royal Chapel of St Peter ad Vincula, an innocent victim of court intrigue and marital revenge.

# BOLEYN, JANE, COUNTESS ROCHFORD

After the execution of her husband, George, for which she had been almost directly responsible, Countess Rochford continued the duties she had performed as one of Anne Boleyn's personal staff to those who replaced her late mistress, namely Queens Jane Seymour, Anne of Cleves and ultimately Katherine Howard. In 1541 she accompanied the latter on a royal tour around the country, the purpose of which was to allow the public to see and welcome Henry VIII and his new bride. However, her role as Lady of the Bedchamber became more meaningful than the original job description intended, for at various stages of the prolonged excursion she arranged clandestine sessions for Queen Katherine and the Queen's cousin and lover, Thomas Culpepper, sessions which, it was rumoured, sometimes even included Jane herself, beds in the great houses visited by the royal party being capacious enough to accommodate three people.

Following the return of the royal party to Hampton Court, Henry found out about the illicit liaisons and, no doubt exclaiming the Tudor equivalent of, 'Oh no, not again!' accompanied by suitable expletives, put the standard procedure into operation. One of those arrested was the Countess, who was charged with concealing the Queen's infidelity with Culpepper and others, a crime amounting to treason. She was confined in Sion House, near Hampton Court. There, the prospect of her inevitable fate proved too much for her stability and she went out of her mind.

On 21 January 1541 she was attainted (condemned without trial) by Parliament and, nursed back to only partial normality, on Friday 10 February she was taken along the River Thames from Sion House, entering the Tower via Traitors' Gate. Three days later, at eight o'clock in the morning, Jane Rochford mounted the scaffold on Tower Green where, only six years before, her husband had also stood. Penitent at last, she confessed that 'her end was a punishment for having contributed to her husband's death by false accusation of Queen Anne Boleyn'. As the pendulum had swung, so did the axe, and now her remains moulder in her tomb beneath the altar in the Tower's chapel beside those of the people she betrayed.

## BRANDRETH, JEREMIAH
## TURNER, WILLIAM
## LUDLUM, ISAAC

Jeremiah Brandreth, together with his friends William Turner and Isaac Ludlam, have a claim to fame they could well have dispensed with, for to them goes the doubtful honour of being the last persons to be beheaded by the axe in this country, as comparatively recently as the year 1817 – beheaded, though not 'executed' (killed) by the axe, that subtle distinction going to Simon, Lord Lovat in 1747.

In 1817 social unrest was rife, insurrection in the air, and while some leaders of riots were transported to the colonies, three Derbyshire men, Brandreth, Turner and Ludlum, were sentenced to death as a terrible example to all potential troublemakers. Nor was the sentence that they be merely hanged; nothing less would satisfy the authorities than that they be hanged, drawn and quartered. However, this horrific fate was mitigated somewhat, the penalty being later reduced to one whereby they would be hanged first, excused the mutilation of being 'drawn and quartered', but then be beheaded after death – not, as was the usual practice, with a knife but, at the insistence of the Prince Regent, with the axe, as the symbol of the dire punishment meted out to traitors. For some unknown reason, the axe held in the Tower was not sent for; instead a local blacksmith manufactured two of the weapons similar to the 'official' one, the blades being eight and a half inches long and twelve inches wide.

On execution day a large and excited crowd gathered round the gallows specially constructed outside Derby gaol, a crowd so large that soldiers and even the cavalry had to be called out to keep sympathizers from crowding too close to the scaffold. Cheers for the doomed 'local heroes' mingled with cat-calls directed at the officials as the three condemned men mounted the platform. But the strident voices were silenced as the nooses tightened and the bodies swung helplessly from the gallows, to be left suspended for an hour to ensure the complete cessation of life, before being cut down.

A long trestle had been placed near the scaffold and on this the first corpse, that of Jeremiah Brandreth, was laid face down, positioned so that the throat rested on a wooden support nailed to one end. A local miner, unrecognizable behind the mask he wore, stepped forward and swung the axe – unsuccessfully. A second attempt was equally ineffective so, in order to separate the head completely from the torso, his assistant completed the decapitation with a knife. But the grisly drama had to be played out to the full. Gripping the severed head by the hair, the axe-wielder, raising it high, loudly proclaimed, 'Behold the head of a traitor, Jeremiah Brandreth!' Whereupon most of the crowd, recoiling in horror at the ghastly sight, took to their heels and fled, leaving but a hardened few, plus the officials and troops, to watch the bodies of Turner and Ludlum being carried to the trestle, there to be similarly maltreated. Among those who remained to the end was the poet Shelley, who later angrily petitioned the authorities, castigating those who, in the name of justice, had defiled their public office. But it was too late, much too late for Brandreth, Turner and Ludlum.

## CAMPBELL, ARCHIBALD, 8th EARL OF ARGYLL
## CAMPBELL, ARCHIBALD, 9th EARL OF ARGYLL

A father and son who suffered the same fate, both bowing low in humble obeisance before the Scottish Maiden.

The 8th Earl, born in 1598, was known as 'Gillespie Grumach' and the 'glae-eyed marquis' because of his pronounced squint. Throughout his life he was a fervent Scottish patriot and in his efforts to preserve his country's independence he initially supported Charles I, but later persuaded the Scottish parliament to sit, in defiance of the King's order. In the political maelstrom of the times, James Graham, the Earl of Montrose, emerged to become his bitter enemy and, in June 1641, was imprisoned for some months by Argyll for slandering him to the King. Ever a man of action, the 'glae-eyed marquis' went on the offensive, leading an army against the Royalist nobles in Perth and Aberdeen and, although routed by Montrose's troops at Inverlochy, later invaded England, getting as far south as Newcastle.

When Oliver Cromwell established the Commonwealth,

Argyll invited him to Edinburgh and became head of the new executive committee. He wasted no time in agreeing to the death sentence imposed on his old foe, Montrose, in May 1650 for supporting Charles I. However, he soon became disillusioned with Cromwell's plans for Scotland and encouraged Charles II to come to Scotland from the Continent, even placing the crown on his head in January 1651. Realizing, however, that he did not have the full confidence of the King, he resumed his alliance with Cromwell, becoming Member of Parliament for Aberdeenshire in the Commonwealth Parliament in 1658. When, two years later, public opinion swung against their political masters and called for the restoration of the monarchy, Argyll came south to London and welcomed Charles II – to be promptly arrested and charged with high treason.

In May 1661 Archibald Campbell who, together with his wife had gloated over the spectacle of the Earl of Montrose being hanged, drawn and quartered, was himself sentenced to death. Not for him the rope and the dismembering knife, however; he was forced instead to submit to the blade of the Scottish Maiden, and his severed head was then carried by the executioner to the roof of Edinburgh's Tolbooth, there to replace that of his erstwhile enemy, Montrose.

The Marchioness of Argyll had lost her husband, but worse was to follow, for her son Lord Lorn, succeeding to the title as 9th Earl of Argyll in 1663, ultimately followed the same dread route along Canongate and High Street to where the Maiden would claim his head.

Archibald junior was a more dedicated Royalist than was his father, and when all was lost and Charles I was executed, he became captain of Charles II's Bodyguard in 1650 and did his best to muster armed support from the clans in that year. But as the months passed the King urged him to bide his time and co-operate with Cromwell. This he did, but probably continued to conspire with the Royalists, for in August 1656 he was arrested and, in the following year, imprisoned in Edinburgh Castle until being released when Charles II was restored to the throne.

Archibold then became involved in political intrigues, as had his father, and in 1680 he opposed the arbitrary measures proposed by the King's brother James, Duke of York, who was then High Commissioner for Scotland. Within months he was accused of treason, sentenced to death and confined in Edinburgh Castle. However, in 1682 he managed to escape disguised as a page, holding the train of his stepdaughter, Lady Sophia Lindsay – a near-run thing, for it was reported that as they were going out, a sentry grasped Argyll's arm, causing him to panic and drop the end of the train. Reacting with astonishing presence of mind, Sophia saved the situation by taking hold of the train and striking her 'page' with it, thereby smearing his face with mud and snow, and exclaiming, 'Thou careless loon!'

One of Archibald's servants, a man named Spence, was arrested and closely questioned by Lord Perth and members of the Scottish Council. Reluctant to incriminate his master, Spence was threatened with being tied in a chair and put to a traditional Scottish torture, the 'Boots'. One version of this consisted of narrow boards being strapped tightly to each side of the victim's legs, which were next tied tightly together. Wedges were then hammered between wood and flesh, causing agonizing pain as muscles, flesh and sinews were crushed, leg bones splintered, until the victim was totally crippled. In his book *History in his Own Time* written in 1823, Bishop Burnet reported that this method of persuasion was considered by contemporary observers to be the most severe and cruel pain in the world. So dreadful to watch, in fact, 'that when any are struck in the boot, it is done in the presence of the Council and upon that occasion almost all offer to run away'. For that

reason an order was issued to compel a quorum to stay, otherwise a confession would not be classed as valid. However, one
man who would not have missed the fearful spectacle for
anything was James, Duke of York. Never noted for his caring
and tender nature, he was 'so far from running away that
he looked on all the while with an unmoved indifference and
with an attention as if he were watching a curious experiment.
This gave a terrible impression of him to all that observed it,
as a man that had no bowels of humanity in him,' wrote the
Bishop.

Somehow the servant managed to endure the agony as the
mallet drove the wedges deeper and deeper between the
boards and his flesh and, despite further measures being
taken to extract a confession, he did not yield until the thumb-
kins – the thumbscrews – compressed his thumb-nails and
brought about his surrender. By then it was too late, for his
master had fled the country. Travelling via London, Archibald
made his way to Holland, from where he actively conspired
with the Rye House Plotters, a group planning to ambush the
King and the Duke of York at Rye House Farm in
Hertfordshire as they returned from the races, assassinate
them and place James, Duke of Monmouth on the throne.
Being involved in this conspiracy brought about his downfall
for, following the disastrous Monmouth Rebellion and the
consequent brutal executions ordered by Judge Jeffreys, he
was taken prisoner in June 1685 and again sentenced to
death.

This time there was no escape. On the day of his execution
he gave a farewell dinner to his friends before being escorted
to the High Council House. There, while the workmen erected
the stands and barriers necessary to control the vast crowds,
he wrote a final letter to his wife, before being conducted to
where the Scottish Maiden waited. With great composure he
knelt and positioned his neck between the two uprights,

commenting that the machine was 'a sweet maiden whose embrace will waft my soul to heaven'. A swift sign to the executioner – a brief rumbling sound as the weighted blade travelled down the grooves – and his severed head fell into the waiting basket. After being parboiled it was taken to the Tolbooth, where it replaced that of his father which, for thirty-five years, had scowled down on those passing along the busy streets below. A patriotic Scotsman to the very end, Archibald Campbell, 9th Earl of Argyll, has the doubtful claim to fame in that he was the last person to be decapitated by the Scottish Maiden.

## CAPEL, ARTHUR, BARON OF HADHAM

In the peaceful cemetery of St Cecilia's Church at Little Hadham, Hertfordshire, the soft wind sighs through the trees and the peacocks shriek their mournful cry. Within the fourteenth-century building the remains of Lord Capel rest in the family vault under the altar, beneath an inscription which reads; 'Hereunder lieth interred the body of Arthur, Lord Capel, Baron of Hadham, who was murdered for his loyalty to King Charles the First, March 9th 1649.'

Arthur Capel, born about 1610, was Member of Parliament for Hertfordshire by the age of thirty and became a fervent supporter of Charles I, being appointed the King's lieutenant-general in Shropshire, Cheshire and, three years later, North Wales. In the politically turbulent days of 1646, Capel escorted the Queen to Paris where she would be out of danger and, a few months later, assisted the King himself to escape from imprisonment in Hampton Court Palace. With other Royalists he fought courageously to rescue the situation which was getting more desperate by the hour, but finally his forces were overrun at Colchester. When that city surrendered in August

1648, he was captured and taken to Windsor Castle, from where he was later transferred to the Tower of London. Charged with high treason, he and many fellow Royalists awaited trial –a trial which could have no other outcome than being sentenced to death. But Arthur Capel had no intention of giving up hope, of meekly accepting the inevitable; if death was the only alternative, what had one to lose? So he decided to escape.

In the seventeenth century the Tower was a top security prison. All its portals were protected by drawbridges strongly guarded by Yeoman Warders and the soldiers of the garrison. Moreover, it was surrounded by its moat, a thirty-yard-wide ditch with muddy sloping sides, twelve to fifteen feet deep, the indescribable filth of the city which drained into it forming its stagnant, semi-solid depths, its slimy waters rarely disturbed except by the infrequent opening of Traitors' Gate. Escape on foot was out of the question, nor could Lord Capel swim; but thinking positively, he listed his assets. He was tall – well above six feet in height; friends had told him of a route across the moat which they thought might be less deep than elsewhere, probably where more solid rubbish had been dumped; and they were prepared to smuggle in ropes and grappling irons wrapped round their bodies beneath their cloaks. The rest was up to him.

Fortunately, he was confined in a tower less well guarded than others, and so one misty night he managed to mount the battlements, secure the hook to a rail and lower himself into the moat below. Gingerly he stepped out into the soft mud, the weed-covered water coming up to his chin. Never knowing whether the next step would plunge him into a sudden hollow, the stench from the bubbles disturbed by his feet almost overpowering him, he swayed on tiptoe to maintain his balance, fearing all the time that in the blackness of the night he had perhaps veered off course and was staggering round the moat instead of crossing it. To return to where the axe awaited was out of the question, even assuming he could locate the rope left hanging from the walls. Losing all track of time, he was on the point of collapse when suddenly one foot struck harder ground; he heard the frantic voices of his friends encouraging him to make one final effort; then felt their arms seize him and drag him up the bank and into the waiting coach.

His rescuers took him to a sympathizer's house where, bathed and changed, he slowly recuperated after his appalling ordeal. But the hunt for the escaped prisoner, concentrated on the City, became so threatening during the following two or three days that it was decided to smuggle him to a 'safe house' further along the river, out on Lambeth Marsh. Accordingly one night he and his companions, all heavily cloaked, hailed a ferry boat at Temple Steps (now Temple Pier on the Embankment) and headed downstream. But it was then, just when freedom seemed within Capel's grasp that, unknown to anyone in the party, everything went horribly wrong. The ferryman happened to hear one of his passengers address his taller companion as 'My Lord'. Only too aware of the hue-and-cry in the City and the much publicized description of the escaped prisoner; aware too of the substantial reward offered for information leading to his capture, he continued to row the men to their destination. After they had disembarked at Lambeth Pier he tied up his vessel and surreptitiously followed them, noting the address of the house they entered. Then, as described in Heath's *Chronicle*: 'Having watched them to the house, he went and bargained for his discovery. His Lord being accordingly seized, was returned on the next day to the Tower, and his betrayer, though rewarded by Parliament, became the scorn and contempt of everybody, and lived afterwards in shame and misery.'

At his subsequent trial on 8 March 1649, 'in a thin house,

hardly above sixty being there' Lord Capel defied the judges, claiming that:

> in the condition and capacity of a soldier and a prisoner of war, the lawyers and gownsmen had nothing to do with him; he insisted that the law of nations exempted all prisoners from death if it were not inflicted within so many days, and that time had long expired, and that if he had committed any offence worthy of death he ought to be tried by his peers, which was his right by the laws of the land.

But his implacable enemy Henry Ireton, Cromwell's son-in-law and signatory to Charles I's death warrant, overruled him, and the president of the court, John Bradshaw, who had pronounced the King's death sentence, bluntly informed Capel that he would be tried by whomsoever the court thought fit.

When Lady Capel presented her petition on her husband's behalf, many members of the court, even Oliver Cromwell himself, spoke favourably, the latter adding however that his, Cromwell's, affection towards the public much outweighed his private friendship towards Capel. 'Furthermore,' he said, 'he had great courage, industry and generosity, so he had many friends who would always adhere to him and as long as he lived, whatsoever condition he might be in, he would always be a thorn in their sides. He therefore, for the good of the Commonwealth, should give his vote against the petition.'

So Arthur Capel was found guilty of high treason and sentenced to death. Ironically, Bradshaw and Ireton, who had spoken so vehemently against him, both died before the Restoration of the Monarchy and were buried with great pomp and ceremony in Westminster Abbey, but when Charles II returned to the throne their corpses were dug up and, together with that of their leader Oliver Cromwell, taken to Tyburn where they were hanged and decapitated, their heads then adorning the roof of Westminster Hall for many years to come.

On 9 March 1649 a platform was erected in New Palace Yard in front of Westminster Hall and Arthur Capel, his death sentence by hanging having been commuted to the more honourable one of being beheaded, walked through the Hall, saluting his friends, his countenance serene and untroubled. Lord Clarendon in his *History* describes him as wearing 'a sad-coloured suit, his hat cocked up and his cloak thrown under his arm'. On ascending the platform, he bowed, gave his hat to his servant and with a clear and manly voice delivered a speech vindicating the cause of the late monarch and urging the people to serve their present King (Charles II, in exile) as their true and lawful sovereign.

Turning to face Richard Brandon who, it is believed, had been the executioner of King Charles I only five weeks previously and was doubtless using the same weapon, Arthur Lord Capel knelt over the block, gave the sign – and the axe descended, to sever the head 'at one choppe off!'

# CHARLES I

In the early 1640s the power struggle between Kingly prerogative and Parliamentary privilege, and the question of the despotic Sovereign's right to raise taxes without consulting the Commons reached fever pitch. The Members, backed by public opinion, were gaining the upper hand and the subsequent Civil War between the Royalists and the Parliamentary forces eventually resulted in victory for the latter. The King could have been deposed, even sent into exile abroad, but on 9 January 1648 (old style; until 1752 the Julian Calendar was in use, New Year's day being 25 March) a Sergeant-at-Arms rode up the middle of Westminster Hall and, to a flourish of trumpets, proclaimed that the Commons of England had resolved to bring King Charles I to solemn trial.

Accordingly, on 20 January, after lengthy hearings, the inevitable verdict of guilty was delivered, the findings and sentence were confirmed by the Commons, who ordered that the execution axe be brought from the Tower in readiness. The Warrant itself was brutal and unambiguous:

Whereas Charles Stuart, King of England, is and standeth convicted of High Treason and other High Crimes; and sentence upon Saturday last was pronounced against him by this Court, to be put to death by the severing of his head from his body; of which Sentence execution yet remaineth to be done. These are therefore to will and require you to see the said Sentence executed, in the open Street before Whitehall, upon the morrow, being the thirtieth day of this instant month January between the hours of Ten in the morning and Five in the afternoon, with full effect. And for so doing, this shall be your Warrant. And these are to require all Officers and Soldiers and other Good People of the Nation of England, to be assisting unto you on this Service.

Given under our Hands and Seals, John Bradshaw, Thomas Grey, Oliver Cromwell [and fifty-six others].

On the terrible day on which the King was sentenced to die, the execution was delayed. Although food had been prepared for him, Charles was determined that all he would partake of would be the bread and wine of the Holy Sacrament. Noon came and his spiritual adviser, Bishop Juxon, urged him to eat. The weather was bitterly cold, and without any nourishment, Charles would be even more liable to tremble on the scaffold; his voice would quiver when addressing his subjects for the last time, thereby giving them the impression that his hitherto dauntless spirit had been broken. Reluctantly, Charles admitted the wisdom of the cleric's words. Normally a hearty eater, and despite being by now extremely hungry, he only ate half a manchet, a small bun-shaped loaf, and drank a glass of claret. Thus fortified, he patiently awaited the arrival of what was to be, in effect, his cortège.

He was escorted from St James's Palace to the Banqueting House in Whitehall by a Regiment of Foot with flags flying and drums beating, and also members of the Yeomen of the Guard. He was dressed in a suit of black satin with a short velvet coat, his sombre dress contrasting with the gold cane he carried. Meanwhile, another leading player in the drama that was being enacted, the public executioner, believed to be Richard Brandon, having shown some hesitancy at his coming role, was 'fetched out of bed by a troop of horse and escorted to the scaffold site'.

At 2 pm the King was conducted through one of the large windows of the Banqueting House on to a large black-draped platform which projected out into Whitehall, a dais visible to the thousands who packed the streets and surrounding windows, some even clinging to rooftops and chimneys.

Two masked men dressed entirely in black now awaited the King, one seemingly old, the other a young fair-haired man. Such was the aversion felt by so many at the actual decapitation of a king, whatever his dissolute or arrogant ways, that the executioners had taken precautions, disguising themselves to avoid future reprisals. Their masks and false beards, together with thick coats, were so effective that at the Restoration of the Monarchy eleven years later, vengeful Royalists accused a captain in the Commonwealth Army, William Hewlet, of being one of those responsible. There is little doubt, however, that it was Brandon who waited for his victim that day, his assistant being William Lowen, a former dung-hill cleaner.

On the scaffold, the King presented Sir Thomas Herbert with his silver alarm watch; to Bishop Juxon he gave a gold medal mint-mark, probably that of a £5 or £6 piece, which had been submitted to him for approval of the design of his head, which would appear on the coin, ironically the head which moments later would be severed from his body, and also the 'George', the jewel of the Order of the Garter. All these relics survived, together with the handkerchief he used at the time, in fine white cambric, marked with the crown and initialled 'C.R.', the shirt and drawers worn by the King, and the sheet which was thrown over his remains.

While speaking to the cleric he noticed one of those near him reach out and touch the axe. Fearful that any handling could blunt its edge, and also recalling the agonizing death suffered by his grandmother Mary, Queen of Scots, two blows with the axe having been delivered before her head was severed, he exclaimed, 'Hurt not the axe, that it may not hurt me!' Then, on seeing that the block was only ten inches high, objected strongly, for it would require him to lie humiliatingly prone instead of kneeling. This was confirmed by an eyewitness quoted in the *Moderate Intelligencer* dated 1 February 1648/9 who stated that 'the block was a little piece of wood, flat at bottom, about a foot and a half long.' Brandon replied, 'It can be no higher, Sir,' omitting to explain also that the low block and the four staples driven into the surrounding boards were there to facilitate binding the King into the necessary position, should he refuse to submit.

Charles then told Brandon not to strike until he gave the signal by stretching out his arms, to which the executioner replied, 'I will, an't please Your Majesty.' The white satin cap was next donned, the King saying to Brandon, 'Does my hair trouble you?' Because it was essential that the target, the nape of the King's neck, was not obscured, Bishop Juxon assisted the man to tuck all the flowing locks under the cap. Finally, the

King urged Brandon to do his work cleanly and not put him to pain, but the executioner, evidently overcome by the enormity of his task, could only nod his head.

Charles lay down full length and, positioning his neck on the block, started to pray. Suddenly he realized that Brandon was standing over him, the axe poised high in readiness. 'Wait for the sign – wait for the sign!' he exclaimed loudly. There was a pause, then the King spread his arms wide: simultaneously Brandon reacted, bringing the weapon down with crushing force. Quoting a shocked eyewitness in his book *Romance of London*, published in 1835, John Timbs wrote: 'Then sodanly with one bloe his head sped from his shoulders, and a universal groan, the like never heard before, broke from the dense and countless multitude.' The horror was further intensified when the assistant hangman Lowen picked up the severed head and, displaying it to the massed spectators, shouted, 'Behold, the head of a traitor!'

After the execution, Charles's head and body were placed in a coffin and conveyed to the late King's sleeping quarters in the Palace of Whitehall, a slanderous story later being circulated that Oliver Cromwell inspected the cadaver and lifted the head to confirm that it had indeed been severed from the torso!

The corpse was embalmed by Dr Trapham, a Maidstone practitioner who had been promoted Surgeon-General by the new regime. Such was the authorities' haste to close the grim chapter, the doctor had to forego the usual slow and painstaking method of embalming for a quicker one. Accordingly he started by removing 'all those parts which were disposed to corruption', i.e. the internal organs, and discovered that the King's vital parts were in excellent condition, no disease whatsoever being apparent.

In compliance with the existing rules, which stipulated that 'after emptying the cavities, surgeons should work on the head', Dr Trapham drained the blood from the severed head, then performed a trepanning operation, sawing off a section of the skull in order to remove the brain. The cavity was then washed out with aromatic wine and filled with cotton and flax soaked in liquid balsam, after which he replaced the section of the cranium and carefully joined up the incised skin with needle and surgical thread.

Turning his attention once again to the body, the doctor drained the blood away in a similar manner, this time by severing the veins and arteries, subsequently filling all the cavities with powder of aloe and myrrh. Having sponged all the moisture from the skin, he then applied liquid balsam as a preservative before swathing the body tightly with linen bandages. And having completed that task, he sewed the head back into position on the mutilated trunk.

After being displayed to the public in St James's Palace, the coffin was taken to Windsor Castle, five mourning coaches following the ordinary hearse, the snow falling so heavily that by the time the cortege reached its destination the black velvet pall had been entirely covered with it. White, the colour symbolically worn by a victim, was considered an omen of ill luck for Charles as early as his coronation, when he wore robes of white velvet instead of the traditional red or purple. The astrologer William Lilley blamed it on the 'indirect and fatall advise of William Laud, Archbishop of Canterbury who perswaded the King to apparell himself in a White Garment; there were some dehorting him from wearing the white apparel but he obstinately refused their council.' There was, however, a rational reason for the change of colour, as explained by de Quincey: 'When King Charles came to be crowned, all the stock in London was insufficient to furnish the purple velvet necessary for the robes of the King and for the furniture of the throne. To obtain further supplies from Genoa would delay the coronation by one hundred and fifty days.' A reasonable explanation but one dismissed by the court Cassandras.

The coffin was deposited in the late King's bedroom pending a decision on the actual burial site. St George's Chapel meeting with general approval, the officials paid the fee of five shillings and sixpence to Isaac, the sexton, and Widow Puddifat to unlock the chapel doors. The chosen vault was then located by one of the officials tapping with his staff on the stone floor, hollow sounds identifying their objective.

Gaining entrance, they crouched inside the vault, which was only four feet ten inches high at the centre of the arched ceiling, and found two coffins: one, six foot ten inches in length, made of elm with shreds of a purple pall still attached to its lid, without doubt that of Henry VIII, its disintegrating timbers allowing a glimpse of the skeleton within, a wisp of beard still adhering to its chin; the other, a much smaller one, was that of Jane Seymour, Henry's third wife. While workmen were engaged in cutting 'King Charles, 1648' (old style date) in a lead tablet to be attached to the coffin, the sexton reported that he had caught a foot-soldier in the chapel 'who had cut so much of Henry VIII's velvet pall as he judged would hardly be missed, and wimbled a hole in the coffin, probably fancying that there was something there, well worth his adventure.' He, the sexton, said he had detained the sacrilegious person and on searching him, 'a bone from the coffin was found on him which, the man admitted, he would have made into a knife haft.' One hopes the souvenir was replaced with the rest of Henry's remains.

With the lead tablet secured in place on its lid, Charles's coffin was brought from the Castle bedroom. Colonel Witchcott, Governor of Windsor Castle, having forbidden that a burial service be held, it was placed next to the other two coffins and a black velvet pall draped over it before the vault was once more sealed up. In contrast to the vast sums of money incurred at other royal funerals, the cost of Charles I's interment amounted to a mere £229 5s.

One hundred and sixty-five years later, on 1 April 1813, the vault was again opened and entered. The Prince Regent was present, as were the Duke of Cumberland, Count Munster, the Dean of Windsor and Sir Henry Halford, physician to the King, George III. A square opening was cut in the upper part of the lead coffin large enough to enable the visitors to see that inside was a wooden coffin, very much decayed, and inside that the body, wrapped in cere-cloth. Sufficient of this covering was removed to reveal the face, immediately recognizable as that of Charles I, the appearance being as perfect as when he had been alive, the oval shape of the head and the pointed beard identical to those in the van Dyck portraits.

Sir Henry later reported:

When the head had been entirely disengaged from the attachments which confined it, it was found to be loose, and without any difficulty was taken up and held to view. The hair was thick at the back of the head and in appearance nearly black. A portion of it, which has since been cleaned and dried, is of a beautiful dark brown colour. That of the beard is of a redder brown. On the back of the head it was more than an inch in length and had probably been cut so short for the convenience of the executioner or by the surgeon when sewing the head back in place.

On holding up the head to examine the place of separation from the body, the muscles of the neck had evidently retracted themselves considerably; and the fourth cervical vertebra was found to be cut through its substance transversely, leaving the surfaces of the divided portions perfectly smooth and even, an appearance which could have been produced only by a heavy blow inflicted with a

very sharp instrument, and which furnished the last proof
wanted to identify King Charles I.

The fissure made by the axe was clearly visible, the flesh at its
edges blackened and torn, the back of the head and the place
where it rested in the coffin being stained with what was obviously blood. Sir Henry did not include everything in his report,
omitting all mention of a deplorable scene which had taken
place. As mentioned above, the doctor had originally sewn the
head back on to the trunk and so the two body parts had to be
separated before the head could be lifted out of the coffin.
Some stitches had to be cut, others came away. And on lifting
the head, the assistant, understandably nervous and excited,
dropped the head on the stone floor – whereupon the Prince
Regent swore at him and walked out!

Relieved of the royal presence, the rest of the party seem to
have lost all sense of decency; behaving like ghouls they
proceeded to help themselves to souvenirs, robbing the corpse
of hair and chips of bone, one of the visitors even stealing one
of Henry VIII's teeth from the nearby coffin. The royal physician himself cut off a lock of the King's hair and later
presented part of it, set in a golden locket, to the novelist Sir
Walter Scott. A few strands recently re-emerged into the light
of day, being auctioned in April 1995 to a Mr John Reznikoff,
an American gentleman from Stamford, Connecticut, for the
sum of £3910, his collection of hirsute appendages including a
lock of Napoleon's hair (£345) and also strands of Henry IV's
beard (£1265). Where unique souvenirs are concerned, apparently nothing is sacred.

Sir Henry, not content with the lock of hair, also removed
and kept the dead King's fourth cervical vertebra. There are
at least two conflicting accounts of what subsequently
happened to it: one version alleges that, used as a saltcellar
on his dining table, it became a conversation piece for nearly

thirty years until word of the desecration reached Queen Victoria. Her Majesty, far from being amused, ordered it to be returned and so, in a small casket, it was replaced in the tomb within St George's Chapel. The other, perhaps more credible account, is that the bone was passed down through Sir Henry's descendants until it came into the possession of Sir Henry's grandson, also named Sir Henry Halford. He decided that this relic of a King should be returned to the royal family and so he presented it to the Prince of Wales (later King Edward VII), who kept it, enclosed in a small ebony casket, on his private writing desk in Windsor Castle. However, a close personal friend took such a great dislike to it – and was obviously sufficiently privileged to express his or her distaste – that the Prince agreed to have the vertebra returned to the tomb.

This was carried out on 18 December 1888 at dusk after a service in St George's Chapel. A sufficiently large aperture having been made through the floor and the brick archway of the vault, the Prince of Wales, escorted by the Dean of Windsor, Dr Randall Davidson (afterwards Archbishop of Canterbury) and two Canons, carried the bone in its ebony box. Handkerchiefs were knotted together to form an improvised rope and the Prince knelt on the floor, slowly lowering the casket until at last it lay, if not in, at least on the coffin which contained the mortal remains of the King who had been so cruelly executed.


# CONSTABLE, WILLIAM

This eighteen-year-old son of a miller, also known as William Fetherstone, suffered death simply because he lived in the mid-sixteenth century, Queen Mary's reign, rather than in the present, more humane twenty-first century, when his mental problems would have been diagnosed and treated accordingly. On 10 May 1555 he was arrested in Eltham in Kent for proclaiming that Edward VI, Henry VIII's sickly son (who had died aged sixteen three years earlier) was still alive; he also insisted at other times that he himself was that King.

He was taken to Hampton Court and, when interrogated by the council, he asked for pardon, explaining that 'he wist not what hee did but had been perswaded by many'. The authorities wasted little time in diagnosing and treating the youth's mental condition; they sent him to the Marshalsea Prison in London where he was imprisoned until 22 May, when he was carried in a cart through the city to Westminster with a notice displayed on his head stating that he had named himself King Edward VI. This was followed by further remedial action in that he was whipped round the Palace, through Westminster into Smithfield, and then banished to the north of the country.

For some reason the cure was totally ineffective for, as reported by the historian Stow in his *Annals*:

The 26 of February 1556 Willi. Constable alias Fetherstone was arraigned in the Guild Hall of London, who had caused letters to bee cast abrode, that king Edward was aliue, and to some he shewed himselfe to be king Edward, so that many persons both menne and women were troubled by him, for the which sedition the said William had bin once whipped and deliuered, as is aforesaid; but now he was condemned, and the 13 March he was drawne, hanged and quartered at Tyborne.

And so yet another pitiful head gazed down unseeing from the Drawbridge Gate of London Bridge.

# CORNELIUS, JOHN

After the Great Fire of London of 1666 had devastated the City, workmen clearing the debris from the narrow streets and demolishing the burnt-out buildings, made a bizarre discovery among the rubble in a cellar in Blackfriars. Stow's *Survey of London* reports:

> They came to an old wall of great thickness, where appeared a kind of cupboard. Which being opened there was found four Pots or Cases of fine pewter, thick, with Covers of the same, and Rings fastened on the top to take up (lift) or put down at pleasure. The Cases were flat before and rounded behind. And in each of them were reposited a human head, inconsumed by the fire, preserved, as it seems, by Art; with the teeth and Hair, the Flesh of a tawny Colour, w'rapt up in black silk, almost consumed. And a certain Substance, of a blackish colour, crumbled into dust, lying at the bottom of the Pots.
>
> One of these Pots, with the Head in it, I saw in October 1703, being in the custody of Mr. Prestbury, then Sope Maker in Smithfield. The Pot was inscribed on the inside of the cover in a scrawling Character – which might be used in the times of Henry VIII – 'J. CORNELIUS'. This Head was without any neck, having short red hair upon it, thick, and it could not be pulled off; and yellow hair upon the temples, a little bald on top, perhaps a Tonsure, the forepart of the Nose sunk, the Mouth gaping, ten sound teeth, others had been plucked out; the skin like tanned leather, the Features of the Face visible. There was one body near it, buried, and without a head, but no other bodies found. The three other Heads had some of the necks joined to them and had broader and plainer Razure; which showed them to be priests. These three

heads are now dispersed. One was given to an Apothecary, another entrusted with the Parish Clerk who, it is thought, got money by shewing of it. It is probable that they were at last privately procured and conveyed abroad and now become Holy Relicks. Who these were, there is no Record as I know of; nor had any of them Names inscribed but one. To me they seem to have been zealous priests or friers executed for Treason, whereof there were many in the Rebellion in Lincolnshire, An. 1538, or others who had denied the King's Supremacy. And here privately deposited by these Black Friers.

Research by the historian Dr Challoner into the head contained in the pot bearing a name confirmed this to be more or less correct. John Cornelius, or Mohun, was born in 1557 in Bodmin, of Irish parents. After studying at Oxford, he went to Rheims and from thence to Rome, where he studied to become a Roman Catholic priest. Dedicated and devoted to his cause, in 1583 he returned to England, to travel the country bringing spiritual guidance and comfort to the persecuted Catholics during the reign of Queen Elizabeth. Constantly hunted by the authorities he, like his brother priests, had to be prepared to conceal himself at a moment's notice in priest holes (secret hiding places ingeniously constructed in country houses, behind panelling, under stairways, even beneath fireplaces) for days on end, without food or water. Cramped and confined in little more than small cupboards, not daring to move or make a sound, they can only be admired for their endurance.

The official searchers, known as pursuivants, were cunning and expert; counting windows from outside the house, then again from inside, might reveal a hidden room; measuring adjoining rooms could disclose secret cavities; panelling would be tapped to identify hollow spaces behind. Should all these measures fail, the pursuivants would loudly discuss their disappointment and intended departure, only to creep back and, impersonating the house servants, tap on the walls and joyfully announce to the fugitives that the coast was clear, that they could now come out, stretch their limbs, eat and drink. Then they would pounce as their wretched starving and thirsty victim emerged from his cramped hiding place.

In April 1594 John Cornelius visited the widow of Sir John Arundel for the purpose of celebrating Mass. While engaged in his ministrations, a servant, either for reward or in obedience of the law, reported the priest's presence to the pursuivants and on their approach, the priest hastily sought refuge in one of the many hiding places. While some of the searchers made much commotion in one part of the house, shouting and knocking loudly on walls, others waited elsewhere, quietly listening as the hours dragged by. And on hearing a muffled cough, they broke down the panelling and arrested the fugitive priest.

As Cornelius was being led away, a relative of the family, Mr Bosgrave, seeing that the captive was bare-headed, put his own hat on the priest's head, a charitable action which immediately resulted in his own arrest. Two of the house servants, Terence Carey and Patrick Salmon, were also taken into custody for failing to report the presence of the priest themselves.

John Cornelius was taken to London and there racked in an attempt to persuade him to reveal the whereabouts of other Jesuit priests. On his refusal, he was tried and found guilty of high treason. At Dorchester on 2 July 1594, Bosgrave, Carey and Salmon were hanged; Cornelius was hanged, drawn and quartered. It was reported that his head was used as a football by the bigoted mob before being displayed over the city's gate, where it remained for some time until removed after protests by the townsfolk. By devious means the head was then procured by fellow Catholics who presented it to the Black Friars in London as a holy relic. There, stored with others in the crypt, it was revered until, more than seventy years later, the Great Fire reduced the buildings to rubble, leaving the caskets unscathed underground.

# CROMWELL, OLIVER

Following the overthrow in 1649 of the Royalists led by Charles I, Cromwell and his Parliamentary Party ruled the country. The Lord Protector, as Cromwell designated himself, died of gall-stones on 2 September 1658 and was buried with splendour befitting a king in Westminster Abbey.

Two years later the Restoration of the Monarchy brought Charles II to the throne and fearful retribution was levied against those who had passed sentence of execution on the monarch's father. Death being considered no exemption, Cromwell's corpse was rudely exhumed, the mason's receipt for disinterring the cadaver together with those of his two henchmen stating: 'May, the 4th day, 1661. Received then in full of the worshipful Serjeant Norfolke, fourteen shillings for taking up the corps of Cromell, and Ierton and Brasaw. Recd. by mee, John Lewis.'

With the others, Cromwell's corpse was taken to Tyburn and there hanged until sunset, when the head was struck off with an axe and the body buried beneath the gallows. An item published in *The Times* of 9 May 1860 reported that during excavations at the Tyburn site, workmen uncovered a quantity of bones. Since the cadavers of those who had swung on Tyburn Tree were taken away for dissection or display, it is possible that those unearthed could have been the remains of the three Roundheads buried there nearly two hundred years before.

After decapitation, Cromwell's head was impaled on a pike which was then fixed on the roof of Westminster Hall, and

71

there it remained for over forty years until it was blown down in the great gale of 1703. It was then found by a sentry who smuggled it home and concealed it in the chimney, only revealing the fact to his wife on his deathbed. Shortly afterwards she sold it to Herr du Puy, a museum owner who exhibited it in about the year 1710.

It then passed into the ownership of a family named Russell, near relatives of Cromwell who lived in Cambridge, and Samuel Russell, described as a 'poor comedian', offered it to Cromwell's old college, Sidney Sussex, in that city. They declined the offer and so Samuel callously exhibited the head in Covent Garden, charging the public a fee to view it but, in 1787, sold it for £118 to another showman, James Cox or Fox who proceeded to advertise it as 'The Real Embalmed Head of the Powerful and Renowned Usurper Oliver Cromwell', and exhibited it at 5 Mead Court, Old Bond Street, tickets priced at half a crown (2s 6d). By 1812 the head had been sold for £230 to three nieces who, doubtless growing unhappy with their bizarre purchase, sold it to their family physician, Dr Josiah Wilkinson.

From him the head passed to a Mr W.A. Wilkinson, probably a descendant, of Beckenham, Kent, the gory trophy still in the identical box in which it had been placed by the Russells and still in a fair state of preservation, although the nose was flattened to the right side of the face, probably as a result of it falling from the roof of Westminster Hall, and the skull was still pierced by the iron blade of the pike. It remained the possession of the Wilkinsons, being loaned in the 1920s and 1930s for detailed checks to be carried out by eminent antiquaries and experts by means of X-rays and measurements. Comparisons were also made with portraits, sculptures and death masks, one copy of the latter having been owned by Sir Richard Tangye in the nineteenth century. Their conclusions were that the head, of size six and seven-eighths, with a brain capacity of 1500 cubic centimetres, was that of a man aged about sixty who had been decapitated after death, whose skull had earlier been trepanned for embalming purposes and who had the impression of a wart above the eye socket, these findings leaving no doubt as to the authenticity of the head's identity. Moreover it was known that the Lord Protector had foresworn shaving during his daughter's illness, and the bristles were still in evidence on the tightly drawn flesh.

If further proof were needed, the then Master of the Tower Armouries, Charles ffoulkes, confirmed that the remains of the pike were indeed those of a seventeenth-century fighting weapon and had been *in situ* for many decades, the evidence being a worm-hole which penetrated both the skull and the broken shaft.

After World War II the Wilkinsons bequeathed the head to Cromwell's old college, Sidney Sussex, in Cambridge. There, on an oval plaque at the left-hand side of the chapel entrance, are inscribed the words: 'Near to this spot was buried on 25 March 1960 the head of OLIVER CROMWELL Lord Protector of the Commonwealth of England, Scotland and Ireland. Fellow Commoner of this College 1616–17.'

After over three hundred years of ignominious handling, display and abuse, the head of Oliver Cromwell had finally received a Christian burial.

## CROMWELL, THOMAS, EARL OF ESSEX

When Thomas Cromwell proposed a method by which King Henry VIII could divorce Catherine of Aragon in order to marry Anne Boleyn, His Majesty was so pleased that he bestowed many royal favours on his minister. Henry was equally delighted when Cromwell suggested that, by suppressing the monasteries and abbeys, his master would not only destroy the power wielded by the abbots and bishops but could also replenish the royal coffers by confiscating their wealth – and was rewarded with further honours. Again, when the ambitious minister ruthlessly initiated the mass executions of those who dared to protest against the Dissolution, His Majesty showed his appreciation by awarding him even more titles and prestigious posts. When, however, being no judge of feminine pulchritude, Cromwell recommended a decidedly unattractive woman to be his royal master's wife, Henry had him beheaded.

Thomas Cromwell was born about 1485, the son of a blacksmith, in Putney, Surrey, and while still in his teens, went to France. Poverty-stricken he joined the army of the Duke of Bourbon as a common foot-soldier though, being highly intelligent, he was obviously destined to improve his way of life for he is reported to have taught himself Latin by learning the New Testament by heart. This qualification stood him in good stead when he returned from the Continent, enabling him to obtain a position in the household of Cardinal Wolsey. He rose rapidly in that hierarchy, attaining the rank of steward, then secretary and he finally became a solicitor. Parliament beckoned and, as Member for Taunton, his reputation spread until, inevitably, he came to the attention of Henry VIII. The King interviewed him in the royal gardens at Westminster and, recognizing his potential, immediately retained him in his service. By 1531 Cromwell was Privy Councillor, by 1532 Master of the Jewel House and, a few months later, Chancellor of the Exchequer. More honours followed with breathtaking speed. In 1534 Thomas became Baron Cromwell of Oakham in Rutland, with the additional posts of Principal Secretary of State and Master of the Rolls; two years later he was further elevated to the positions of Keeper of the Privy Seal and Vicar General, the latter post giving him the opportunity to have the Bible published in the English language, thereby enforcing every church to have a copy with which to spread its doctrines. No doubt his cup was full to overflowing when, in 1539, he reached the very pinnacle of his career on being appointed Lord Great Chamberlain of England.

Understandably, his popularity rating at court was abysmally low. The Popish party loathed him for his subservience to Henry and also because of the reformation he had promoted, styling him 'Malleus Monachorum', the 'Hammer of the Monasteries'. By the old nobility he was regarded as a Johnny-come-lately, the boss's blue-eyed boy, but such was his influence with the King, few dared criticize him openly. He cared little for those who had suffered by the Dissolution of the Monasteries; the inevitable closure of the hospitals and poorhouses attached to them resulted in the streets of London being flooded with paupers and the sick, their numbers further increased by the hundreds of peasants from the countryside who had until then worked in those religious establishments. Draconian laws were enacted to cope with this influx. If caught living rough or begging they were liable to be arrested and whipped, while scores were shipped like cattle to the newly established colonies in the West Indies and elsewhere.

Determined to make his master supreme in the State and the Church, Cromwell instigated the deaths of opponents such as Sir Thomas More and Archbishop Fisher, endorsed the beheading of Margaret, Countess of Salisbury and those of the abbots and earls who took part in the Pilgrimage of Grace and, in 1536 even escorted Anne Boleyn to the Tower to await her execution. Cromwell's star was indeed riding high – had he not ingratiated himself with his master, suggested and encouraged all the royal decisions from the divorce of Catherine of Aragon onwards? But Fate was lurking in the wings; as wily and calculating as he was, he failed to realize that to maintain the King's friendship, one indispensable condition must be fulfilled – Henry's every enterprise had to be a success. Disappoint him and one's family vault could be opened up and swept out in readiness.

In 1539, following the death of Queen Jane Seymour two years earlier, Cromwell was given the task of selecting a bride for Henry, and so promoted Anne of Cleves (now Kleve, a magnificent walled town near the River Rhine) as a likely candidate to fill the vacancy. Such a union would have forged a strong religious and international link, her father John, Duke of Cleves, being the most influential supporter of Protestantism in Western Germany. But, by concentrating on the political advantages of such a marriage, Thomas had overlooked the intolerable burden he unwittingly inflicted on the King in the unattractive shape and matching appearance of the fraulein, she being described as spotty, thin and tall, of medium beauty and unfashionably dressed; nor could she play any musical instrument. A shrewd political transaction was one thing, but the acceptability or otherwise of the woman with whom one had to live, for Henry in particular, was an entirely different proposition!

Great preparations were made to receive the King's fiancée; palaces were decorated, the mayors of villages between the coast and London warned to organize a goodly turn-out of residents cheering and waving banners. As the King's representative the Earl of Southampton was sent to Calais to escort Anne and, the crossing being delayed by unfavourable weather, the noble Lord had a boring sojourn with the lady in that city, 'Ja!' and 'Yes!' being their only conversation, for she possessed not a word of English and he had no German.

Henry, excited and impatient, decided to meet his future bride at Rochester. On entering the room in which she waited, however, he stopped 'marvellously astonished and abashed'. Forcing himself to embrace her, within minutes he had returned to the royal barge, exclaiming, 'I see nothing in this woman as men report of her, and I marvel that wise men should have made such a report as they have done.' Such a reaction boded ill for the man directly responsible.

The King was diplomatically committed to go through with the marriage ceremony, which took place at Greenwich on 6 January 1540, but he had no intention of enjoying his new wife's company for longer than absolutely necessary. After the wedding Cromwell, consumed with understandable nervousness, asked his master whether he liked her any better, to which Henry exclaimed, 'Nay, my lord, much worse, for by her breasts and belly she should be no maid; which, when I felt them, strake me so much to the heart that I had neither will nor courage to prove the rest!'

The Duke of Norfolk, Thomas's bitter enemy, on seeing the King's barely concealed fury at the impasse into which he had been manoeuvred, seized the opportunity to add tinder to the flames by alleging that Cromwell had passed state secrets to Germany and was also guilty of committing heresy. The fuse had been ignited.

At three o'clock on 10 June of that year Cromwell went to Westminster and finding his colleagues ready to start their meeting in the Council Chamber, commented that they were in a great hurry; as he prepared to sit down and join in he was shocked and horrified to hear the Duke of Norfolk suddenly exclaim, 'Cromwell, do not sit there – traitors do not sit down with gentlemen!' At that signal the captain of the guard and six of his men entered the room and, surrounding Cromwell and ignoring his outraged protests, marched him from the chamber, the jeers and shouts of 'Traitor!' from his erstwhile companions ringing in his ears.

He was taken under escort by river to the Tower where, realizing the terrible implications of his confinement there, he wrote pleading and contrite letters to the King, the first of which was 'writtin with the quaking hand and most sorrowfull harte of your most sorrowfull subject, and most humble servant and prisoner, this Satyrday at the Tour of London'. Another concludes: 'Your Highness's most heavy and most miserable prisoner and poor slave; most gracious prince I cry for mercy, mercy, mercy.' Surprisingly, this abject plea for leniency had so much effect on Henry that he had it read to him three times. However, his desire to rid himself of the 'Flander's Mare' (as he described Anne of Cleves) so that he could marry Katherine Howard, together with the prevailing pressure continually applied by Norfolk, dispelled any thought of clemency. As described by the historian Stow: 'The King's wrath was kindled against all those that were preferrers of this match (to Anne of Cleves), whereof the Lord Cromwell was the chief, for the which, and for dealing somewhat too far in some matters beyond the King's good liking, were the occasions of his hasty death.'

While incarcerated in the Tower he was examined by the Council and on 17 June a Bill of Attainder was levelled against him, its preamble stating that 'the king had raised him from a base degree to great dignities and high trusts, yet he had now, by a great number of witnesses, persons of honor, found him to be the most corrupt traitor and deceiver of the king and crown, that had been known during his whole reign.' He was charged with receiving bribes for selling licences to export money, horses and corn, possessing heretical books and, one with treasonable overtones, planning to marry the Princess Mary, charges on which he was found guilty and sentenced to death.

On the morning of 28 June 1540, 'first calling for his breakfast and therewith eating the same, and after that passing out of the prison downe the hill within the Tower' he mounted the scaffold on Tower Hill, where 'he died patientlie although the executioner was a ragged and butcherly miser who very ungoodly performed the office.'

His body was interred in the royal chapel within the Tower

and his head displayed on London Bridge. Doubtless the happy newly-weds, Henry and Katherine, aboard the royal barge en route from Westminster to Greenwich a few months later, saw the bridge silhouetted against the skyline and could perhaps even make out Cromwell's head as it nodded and rattled on its pike in the wind.

It could be said, however, that Thomas's spirit had the last laugh, for Cromwell had a nephew named Williams, the son of his wife's brother, who had been in the service of Henry VII. During the reign of Henry VIII he was made a member of the Privy Chamber and readopted the family name, becoming Sir Richard Cromwell. One of his descendants was christened Oliver – *the* Oliver Cromwell. So a successor of Thomas, who was beheaded on the orders of a king, avenged his ancestor by himself bringing about the beheading of a later monarch – retaliation indeed!

## CULPEPPER, THOMAS
## DEREHAM, FRANCIS

The grim entry in Tyburn's register of executions for 10 December 1541 reads:

At this tyme the Quene, late before maried to the kyng, called Quene Katheryne, was accused to the Kynge of dissolute liuing, before her mariage, with Fraunces Diram, and that was not secretely, but many knewe it. And sithe her Mariage she was vehemently suspected with Thomas Culpeper, whiche was brought to her Chamber at Lyncolne, in Auguste laste, in the Progresse tyme, by the Lady of Rocheforde, and were there together alone, from a leuen of the Clocke at Nighte till foure of the Clocke in the Mornyng, and to hym she gaue a Chayne and a riche Cap. Vpon this the king remoued to London and she was sent to Sion (House) and there kept close, but yet serued as Quene. And for the offence confessed by Culpeper and Diram, thei were put to death at Tyborne. Culpeper was headed, his body buried at Saint Sepulchers Church by Newgate; Diram was quartered.

While Katherine Howard was yet a teenager she lived in the Duchess of Norfolk's household and, together with other youthful members of the family and staff, proceeded to enjoy herself in the same way as young people have always done. Among the group were two young men, Francis Dereham and Henry Manoc or Mannock. The latter had been employed to teach her to play the spinet and, taking advantage of the young lady's flirtatiousness, had caressed her. Caught in the act by the Duchess, Katherine received a slapping and Madoc was dismissed but, determined to get his revenge, he later passed an anonymous letter to the Duchess informing her of the disgraceful goings-on between her young charge and his successor in her affections, Francis Dereham, a distant relative of the Norfolks. Incensed, the old lady surprised the couple in the gentlewomen's chamber and found them 'in arms, kissing'. She was far from pleased, but little notice was taken of her chidings.

When Henry VIII started to evince an interest in Katherine, Dereham, deciding that discretion was definitely the better part of valour, went to Ireland, where he engaged in a spot of piracy; Katherine, meanwhile, left the Norfolk establishment and entered Court circles at Lambeth, where she met a young cousin named Thomas Culpepper, a man with whom she seemed to fall genuinely in love. Thomas, highly regarded by the King, was a close companion who assisted him to dress, ran personal errands for him, and was at his side for most of the time, holding the appointment of a Gentleman of the

King's Privy Chamber. In that capacity, he was one of the
retinue numbering more than four thousand officials, staff and
guards who formed the 'Progress' planned by Henry VIII after
his marriage to Katherine, a royal tour of the country taken in
order to display his new bride to the populace.

During the tour, Culpepper spent many illicit hours with the
Queen during overnight stops at Lincoln, York and Pomfret,
liaisons connived at and arranged by Jane, Lady Rochford,
Katherine's confidante and companion. Other ladies-in-waiting were also well aware, having literally to be in waiting until
the Queen was eventually ready to retire to bed. Rashly,
Katherine even penned notes to her lover, writing in August:

> Master Culpepper, I heartily recommend me unto you,
> praying you to send to me word how that you do. I did
> hear that ye were sick and I never longed for anything so
> much as to see you. Come to me when Lady Rochford be
> here, for then I shall be best at leisure, to be at your
> commandment . . . trusting to see you again shortly, Yours
> as long as life endures, Katheryn.

Dereham was also back in court circles, having returned from
self-imposed exile and doubtless hoping to resume where he
had left off, only to be warned by the Queen to 'take heed what
words you speak', although at the same time he derived some
encouragement by being appointed Usher of the Chamber to
the Queen.

But the affair with Culpepper couldn't last – those intriguing at court saw to that. Betrayed to Henry, all those
involved were rounded up. First was Dereham, then
Mannock, who admitted that he 'knew a privy mark on the
Queen's body'. Another taken into custody with them was a
man by the name of Damport. It is not known what role he
played, but whatever it was, he sorely regretted it, for in the

Tower he was subjected to 'having his teeth forced out in the brakes', an instrument believed to have resembled a horse's bridle and designed to remove one tooth with agonizing slowness each time an incriminating question remained unanswered. The ultimate fate of Mannock and Damport is not known although it is hardly likely that they were allowed their freedom.

Culpepper and Dereham were tried at the Guildhall on 1 December 1541. Dereham, charged with having had an adulterous affair with Katherine before she was married, confessed openly that 'he had known her carnally many times, both in his doublet and hose between the sheets, and in naked bed,' and that 'he had commonly used to feel the secret and other parts of the Queen's body.' Witnesses were also found who were prepared to swear that Dereham had once said, 'An the King were dead I am sure I might marry her.' At that piece of damning testimony the special commission hardly wasted a moment in finding him guilty and sentencing him to be hanged, drawn and quartered.

Culpepper, on receiving the same verdict and sentence, spoke bravely, albeit recklessly, in his own defence:

Gentlemen, do not seek to know more than that the King deprived me of the thing I love best in the world and, though you may hang me for it, she loves me as well as I love her, though up to this hour no wrong has ever passed between us. Before the King married her, I thought to make her my wife, and when I saw her lost to me, I was like to die. The Queen saw my sorrow and showed me favour, and when I saw it, tempted by the devil, I dared one day while dancing to give her a letter, and received a reply from her in two days, telling me she would find a way to comply with my wish. I know nothing more, my lords, on my honour as a gentleman.

To which Lord Hertford, a member of the commission riposted, 'You have said quite enough, Culpepper, to lose your head!'

In the days that followed, Dereham pleaded desperately for a lesser sentence but was coldly informed that 'the King thinks he has deserved no such mercy'. The only mitigation shown was the council's decision that Culpepper, as a Gentleman of the King's Privy Chamber, would be allowed the privilege of the axe rather than the rope and ripping knife.

There is little more to tell. Both were executed at Tyburn on Saturday, 10 December 1541 – and London Bridge gained two more anatomical ornaments.

## DEVEREUX, ROBERT, EARL OF ESSEX

Could there be any more exalted position in the land than being the favourite of the most powerful woman of her time, Queen Elizabeth I of England? Yet due solely to his own impetuosity and arrogance, Devereux ultimately found himself in a very different position, his neck poised over the block.

He was born in 1567 and at the age of eighteen accompanied his uncle, the Earl of Leicester, fighting in the Battle of Zutphen in Holland where, by his gallant conduct, he was promoted Master of the Horse, becoming a General of Cavalry three years later. After that, recognition at court followed fast, for not only did he receive the Order of the Garter and become a Privy Councillor, but Queen Elizabeth, realizing his talents and impressed by his good looks and attentiveness to her, appointed him Master of the Ordnance and Earl Marshal. His military prowess was again much in evidence when, in 1589, he joined Drake in the expedition to Portugal and, two years later, while serving with the army in Normandy. In 1597, on his return from a second expedition against the Spaniards in the West Indies, he asked for, and was given, the appointment as governor of Ireland, a post that involved quelling the rebels in that country. However, he entered into a dispute with the Queen over the appointment of a deputy some months later. So insolent was his attitude at that time that Elizabeth boxed his ears; whereupon he laid his hand on the hilt of his sword and declared it was an insult which he would not have tolerated from her father (Henry VIII) much less than from a king in petticoats!

Despite all his military expertise it was the insurmountable task posed by Ireland which heralded his eventual downfall. While trying to cope with the difficulties and dangers of the situation, he was surrounded by spies, his every movement watched. In England his enemies at court, jealous of his achievements and the fact that in the past he could do no wrong in the Queen's eyes, were far from idle, directing their most venomous taunts at him. Eventually he could stand no more and, in September 1599, despite Elizabeth warning, 'We do charge you, as you tender our pleasure, that you adventure not to come out of that Kingdom,' in a fit of rage and desperation he returned, hoping that by throwing himself on her mercy he could justify his actions and so retain her favour. But his influence with her had waned so considerably that he was suspended from all his offices except that of Master of the Horse and placed in the custody of the Lord Keeper, forbidden even to communicate with his own wife, despite the fact that she was pregnant.

After some months the Queen partially relented, but Essex, determined to avenge what he considered to be a slight on his integrity, maligned his Sovereign, calling her 'an old woman, crooked in mind and body', and even wrote to James VI of Scotland recommending that he, James, should claim the throne when she died. Not content with verbal abuse, he organized meetings with other malcontents and on 8 February

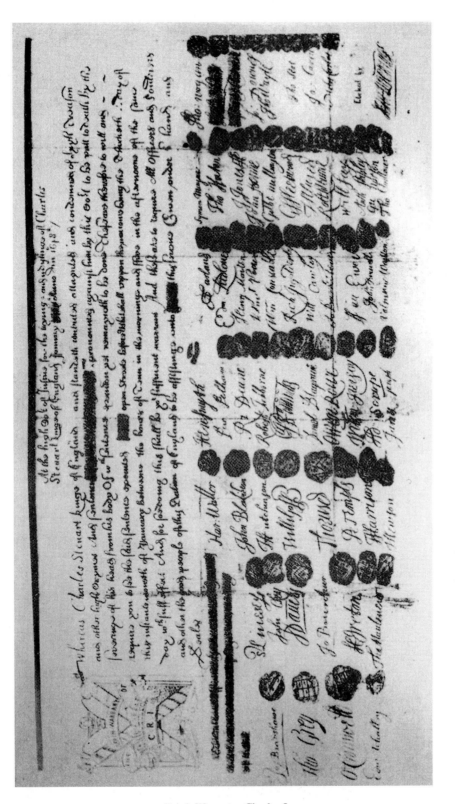

Death Warrant – Charles I

Sir Thomas More's portrait and a portion of his hair shirt

Bell Tower – Sir Thomas More's prison cell

Mary, Queen of Scots *(Above)*

Colonel Barkstead, Regicide
*(Above right)*

Queen Anne Boleyn *(Right)*

Burnt at the Stake

The Gunpowder Plot conspirators

The executioner held the
head on high

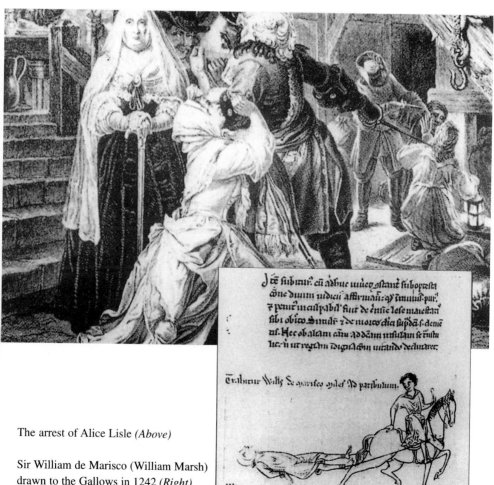

The arrest of Alice Lisle *(Above)*

Sir William de Marisco (William Marsh)
drawn to the Gallows in 1242 *(Right)*

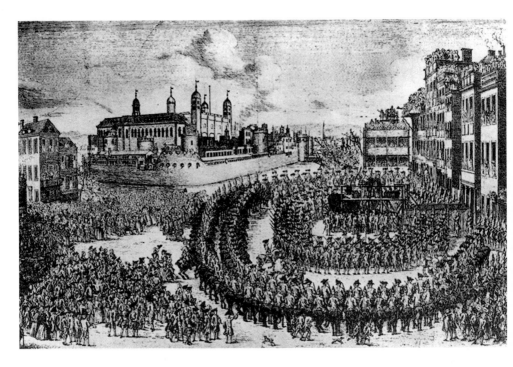

The execution of Lord Lovat on Tower Hill – note collapsing stand

'At One Choppe Off!'

Execution of Lady Jane Grey

Father Arrowsmith's mummified hand *(Left)*

Head of Duke of Suffolk *(Below)*

Head of Oliver Cromwell *(Left)*

1601, leading three hundred armed men, he took the disastrous step of attempting to seize the Tower and the Palace of Westminister with the object of forcing the Queen to dismiss his enemies at court. The attack proved abortive and after a short siege of Essex's town house, he and his supporters were arrested and later charged with having plotted to take away the Queen's crown and life; having conspired how to surprise her at her palace; having broken out into open rebellion and had shut up the lords of the council; and having assaulted the Queen's subjects in the streets.

The trial, which took place in Westminster Hall on 19 February, lasted from nine o'clock in the morning until six in the evening and, as reported by Stow, 'There was a world of people pressing to see the event, and when the news of the condemnation was divulged, many forsook their suppers and ran hastily into the streets to see the Earl of Essex as he returned to the Tower, who went a swift pace, bending his face towards the earth, and would not look at any of them, though some spake directly to him.'

Later, during questioning by members of the government, he confessed all, betraying his erstwhile friends and even admitting that the Queen could never be safe as long as he lived. Elizabeth herself, undecided whether to sign the death warrant or not, vacillated between granting a reprieve because of his impetuous nature and earlier devotion to her, or having him executed because of the enormity of his crime, the insolence of his attitude and his refusal to ask for pardon. At length, after struggling with her emotions, she signed the warrant – then relented – then chiding herself for her indecision, she issued the final order for his death.

On the 25 February 1601, again quoting Stow:

About eight of the clocke in the morning, was the sentence of deathe executed upon Robert Devereux, Earl of Essex, within the Tower of London; a scaffold being set up in the court and a forme neere unto the place whereon sat the earles of Cumberland and Hartford, the lord viscount Bindon, the lord Thomas Howard, the lord Darcy and the lord Compton. The Lieutenant, with some sixteen partisans of the guard [Yeoman Warders], was sent for the prysoner, who came in a gown of wrought velvet, a black sattin sute, a felt hat blacke, a little ruff about his necke, accompanied from his chamber with three divines who he urged to observe him and recall him if eyther his eye, countenance or speech should betray anything which might not beseeme him for that time.

After wishing the Queen a long and prosperous reign, Essex removed his gown and ruff, then prayed, pausing to forgive Derrick, the executioner, whose life, coincidentally, he had saved some years earlier when the man had been condemned to death for a rape at Calais, and whose name was later given to a type of crane which resembled a gibbet.

Having prepared himself spiritually, he lay flat along the scaffold boards and positioned his head upon the low block. Stretching out his arms as the signal to strike, he said, 'Lord, into Thy arms I commend my spirit.' But, as if the trauma of the moment was not enough, the executioner suddenly realized that the collar of Essex's doublet concealed the back of his victim's neck, so Essex had to get to his feet again and take the offending garment off, saying, 'What I must doe, I will doe!' Then, lying with his neck over the block again, he spread his arms wide and bid Derrick to strike, 'and at three strokes he stroke off his head, and when his head was off and in his executioner's hand, his eyes did open and shut as in the time of his prayer; his bodie never stirred, neither any part of him more than a stone, the first stroke howbeit deadly and depriving him of all sense and motion.' As with other unfortunates executed in the Tower, his head and body were then placed in a coffin and buried within the Chapel Royal of St Peter ad Vincula. Meanwhile word of Derrick's inaccuracy with the axe had spread beyond the walls, and on leaving the Tower 'the hangman was beaten, so that the sheriffes of London were called to assist and rescue him from such as would have murdered him.'

It seems that until the very end Devereux assumed he would be reprieved by the Queen, but was Her Majesty waiting to receive a certain token from her erstwhile favourite? According to a well-founded tradition, she had once given him a ring, assuring him that if he were ever in danger and sent it to her, she would receive it as a token of distress and a pleading for pardon, which assuredly would be heard. But the ring somehow fell into the hands of the vengeful Countess of Nottingham and the Queen, her feelings wounded by not receiving it, accordingly ordered the go-ahead for the execution. The deathbed repentance of the Countess of Nottingham and the fearful scene which took place between Elizabeth and the dying woman, who confessed that she had maliciously kept the ring back, are striking incidents in an interesting and dramatic story which, while lacking historical verification, no doubt contains more than the proverbial grain of truth.

## DOUGLAS, JAMES, EARL OF MORTON

If it were true, as tradition has it, that James Douglas, having seen the Halifax Gibbet on one of his journeys to London, actually introduced a similar machine, the Scottish Maiden, into Scotland, there is something exquisitely macabre in the fact that he himself was beheaded by its weighted blade. On the other hand, it could be said that he did himself a favour, for prior to the Maiden, execution was by the sword, a method which did not necessarily guarantee first-time results.

James was born in 1525 and became Earl of Morton in right of his wife. He was appointed Lord High Chancellor by Mary, Queen of Scots, in 1563 and, suspected of involvement in the murder of the Queen's personal secretary, David Rizzio, three years later, took refuge in Northumberland, south of the border, but was later pardoned by Mary. In 1567, aware of the plot to kill Lord Darnley, the Queen's husband, he absented himself from Edinburgh at the crucial time. Establishing his power base and co-operating with Queen Elizabeth, from whom he was receiving bribes, by November 1572 he was appointed Regent but his high-handed attitude towards the other Scottish lords generated a great deal of enmity. Matters came to a head, in more ways than one, for the Earl of Argyll and others persuaded James VI to take over the government from Morton and in 1580 he was accused by the Earl of Lennox of complicity in Lord Darnley's murder. Put on trial, he was found guilty and sentenced to be hanged.

But the King decided otherwise and, on 2 June 1581, he was taken to the Grassmarket in Edinburgh where loomed the Scottish Maiden. After saying, 'Gif I had servit my God as trewlie as I did my King, I had nocht come heir,' he placed his head between the uprights, the restraining bar fell across his neck, the blade was released – and another severed head adorned the top of the nearby Tolbooth.


## ELPHINSTONE, ARTHUR, LORD BALMERINO
## BOYD, WILLIAM, LORD KILMARNOCK
## FRASER, SIMON, LORD LOVAT

The year 1746 witnessed the failure of the Jacobite Uprising, the invading Scots having been driven back over the border and defeated at the Battle of Culloden. Their hero and leader, Prince Charles Edward, the Young Pretender, with the help of Flora MacDonald, had succeeded in getting away in June to the Western Isles and from thence to exile in France. But three who escaped neither capture nor the axe were the Scottish Lords Balmerino, Kilmarnock and Lovat. Brought to London, they were tried, found guilty and sentenced to death. Initially, they were sentenced to be hanged, drawn and quartered as traitors but the sentence was later reduced to one of beheading.

As, even in those days, nothing could be authorized without the necessary chits, a receipt was issued on 11 August 1746 from the Sheriffs' office stating: 'Recd. of John Sharpe Esq. a Writ directing the Sheriffs of London and Middx. to cut off the head of Wm. Earl of Kilmarnock, another to cutt off the head of Arthur Lord Balmerino. signed by me JNO. SAVILE for the Sheriffs of London.'

Accordingly, seven days later, the first two lords, guarded by Yeoman Warders and soldiers, and followed by two hearses carrying their coffins, were escorted from the Tower of London by the Sheriff the short distance to the scaffold on Tower Hill. All had been prepared. At the prisoners' request the block was two feet high, and a thick post had been secured immediately beneath the scaffold to absorb some of the impact of the axe blows. In his official diary, Lieutenant-General Adam Williamson, Deputy Lieutenant of the Tower, necessarily had to report all the macabre details:

A piece of red Bais was supplied in which to catch their heads and not let them fall into the Sawdust and filth of the Stage, and the Earle of Kilmarnock had his head sever'd from the Body at one Stroke all but a little skin which with a little chopp was soon seperated. He had ordered one of his Warders to attend him as his Vallet de Chambre and to keep down the body from strugling or

89

violent Convulsive Motion, but it only flounced backwards on the Seperation of the head and lay on its back, with very little Motion, so that it is probable when ever the head is severd from the Body at one Stroke, it will alwais give that convulsive bounce or spring.

Lord Balmerinos Fate was otherwais, for tho' he was a resolute Jacobite and seemd to have more than ordinary Courage, and indifference for death, yet when he layd his head on the block it is sayd by those on the Scaffold, that when he made his own Signal for decollation, he withdrew his body, so that he had three cuts with the Ax, before his head was severd, and that the by Standers were forc'd to hold his body and head to the block while the Seperation was making.

General Williamson was not the most tactful of men, for he had announced the warrant of execution while Balmerino and his wife were at dinner (wives were admitted to the state prison under those circumstances), whereupon Lady Balmerino promptly fainted. Upon that appalling *faux pas*, her husband exclaimed, 'Lieutenant, with your damned warrant you have spoiled my lady's stomach!'

Simon, Lord Lovat, was not only the last man of the three to face the executioner but was also the last man in English history to be executed by the axe. A man of chameleon-like loyalties, he had fought under Queen Anne, backed the Stuarts against her, deserted again to support the Georges and in 1715 had even opposed the Old Pretender. Detested by many in his own country, he was described by one writer in *The Gentleman's Magazine* dated 17 June 1746 as having 'a fine comely head to grace Temple Bar'.

Renowned for his effervescent sense of humour, when asked by the Major of the Tower how he felt, he replied, 'Why I am about doing very well, for I am preparing myself, Sir, for a place where hardly any majors, and very few Lieutenant Generals go!' A request that he might be executed by the Scottish Maiden in Edinburgh having been rejected by the King, on the fatal day, 9 April, he rose at 5 am and after having a couple of glasses of wine and water, had his wig combed out and later breakfasted on minced veal and more wine and water. In mid-morning he was escorted by the Sheriff to the scaffold on Tower Hill where the crowd, gathering since before dawn, was so enormous that one stand collapsed, killing twenty of the onlookers including the carpenter who had built the stand and his wife who had been selling liquor beneath it. More spectators balanced on rooftops, some even clinging to the rigging of ships moored by the wharf.

On arrival at the scaffold Lovat accepted a drink of burnt brandy and bitters from the Sheriff then, supported by his two Yeoman Warders – he was in his eightieth year and very corpulent – mounted the steps to where John Thrift, the executioner, waited. Surveying the mass of humanity packed round the scaffold he exclaimed, 'God save us! Why should there be such a hustle about taking off an old grey head that can't even get up three steps without three bodies to support it?!'

Presenting Thrift with ten guineas, as was the custom, he felt the edge of the axe then, after a brief prayer, knelt over the block and dropped his handkerchief, the agreed signal. At this, Thrift brought the axe down, severing his head with one blow. It having been decided that none of the Scottish noblemen's heads would be displayed, Lovat's was deposited in the coffin with the torso and carried back into the Tower for burial in the Chapel grounds.

But whether it was or not is somewhat of a mystery, for Lord Lovat's last wish was to be buried in Scotland, and so his cousin had not only arranged for a ship, the *Pledger*, to moor at the Wharf in readiness, but had also engaged Stevenson, a local undertaker, to prepare the body for the journey. However,

Stevenson not only collected the coffin from the Tower but seized the opportunity to benefit from the wide publicity by displaying the cadaver at his funeral parlour in the Strand, charging the public for admission, of course. This entrepreneurial venture continued for some days until the authorities became aware of the scandalous situation and promptly ordered Stevenson to return the corpse to the Tower. Accordingly, a coffin with the appropriate coffin plate attached was duly delivered and then buried within the walls. But whether it contained Lovat's corpse, that of another of Stevenson's customers, or just sand ballast, is open to doubt, for in December 1884 Sir William Fraser, a descendant, claimed that the coffin had in fact been secretly shipped north by night to the Lovat family tomb in Kirkhill near Inverness and that he had recently seen the leaden coffin containing the remains. A poser which would surely have appealed to Simon's sense of humour!

## FAIRBANKE, GEORGE
## FAIRBANKE, ANNA

On 23 December 1623 it was recorded that:

> George Fairbanke, an abandoned scoundrel, commonly called Skoggin because of his wickedness, together with Anna, his spuria [pretended] daughter, were deservedly beheaded by the Halifax Gibbet on account of their manifest thefts. It taking place on market day, as custom demanded, a large crowd of stall holders and townsfolk attended the grim ceremony, having come to complete their Christmas shopping, though many had come into town especially to see the Gibbet Law run its course and to witness the two executions.

# FAWKES, GUY
# WINTER, THOMAS
# ROOKWOOD, AMBROSE
# KEYES, ROBERT

The Gunpowder Plot of 1605, designed to blow up King James I, the Queen and as many of those attending the royal opening of Parliament as possible, is known to most people, but was foiled by an anonymous letter received on 26 October by a Catholic peer, Lord Monteagle, warning him not to attend, for those who do 'shall receyve a terrible blowe'. After due investigation, Guy (or Guido) Fawkes was found by search parties of the Yeomen of the Guard in the vaults beneath the Palace of Westminster on 4 November, with sufficient explosives to cause much destruction and loss of life.

He was taken to the Tower and there persuaded to divulge all he knew about the Plot, the King decreeing that 'if he will not other wayes confesse, the gentler tortour are to be first used unto him *et sic per gradus ad ima tenditur* (and so on, step by step, to the most severe) and so god spede youre goode worke.' Tied to the rack, Fawkes was told that 'he must come to it againe and againe, from daye to daye, till he should have delivered his whole knowledge,' and as the time passed agonizingly slowly, the ratchets clicking, the ropes creaking, threatening to split his joints asunder, it was not long before names, dates and meeting places spilled forth, damning and incriminating his fellow conspirators, all of it written down by his inquisitors, his barely recognizable signature scrawled with his crippled hand.

During the hunt for those he had been forced to betray, some were killed. However, on 27 January 1606 eight of the conspirators, Fawkes, the two Winters, Rookwood, Keyes, Digby, Bates and Grant were taken for trial in Westminster Hall, it being reported that the King and Queen watched the proceedings from a secret place. The prisoners were charged with traitorously conspiring to kill the King, the Queen and Prince Henry, to raise sedition and to produce a miserable slaughter in the realm, to cause rebellion and to subvert and change the government and true worship of God established in the realm, and also to invite foreigners (the Spanish) to invade the realm and make war against the King. Further indictments included 'plotting to blow up the parliament-house with gunpowder; for hiring a house and bringing materials for the purpose, and for taking an oath and the Sacrament for secrecy'. The trial was prolonged, the confessions were read out, the verdicts and sentences inevitable; all were found guilty, all were sentenced to death by being hanged, drawn and quartered.

On Friday, 31 January 1606 Guy Fawkes (whom they call 'the devil in the vault'), Thomas Winter of Hoodington in Warwickshire, Ambrose Rookwood of Stanningfield, Suffolk, and Robert Keyes of London, were drawn from the Tower to Old Palace Yard at Westminster. Winter mounted the scaffold first, where he made a short speech apologizing for his offence and protesting that he died a true Catholic. It was reported that he went up the ladder with a very pale and dead colour and, after a swing or two on the rope, was drawn to the quartering block and there quickly dispatched by the executioner, probably Derrick who, five years earlier, had dispatched Robert Devereux, Earl of Essex.

Thomas Winter was followed by Ambrose Rookwood, who made a long speech confessing his guilt and asking for Divine mercy. He hoped, he said, that the royal family would live long in peace and happiness, but also prayed that God would make the King a Catholic. Beseeching His Majesty to take care of his (Rookwood's) wife and children, he scaled the ladder and, mercifully, was left hanging there until almost dead.

Next came Robert Keyes, who was so impatient to end it all

that he delivered no speech or words of penitence but climbed up the ladder and did not even wait for the executioner to turn it, but leapt off with such force that the rope broke. Immediately he was seized, dragged to the quartering block and there disembowelled and decapitated.

Lastly, Guy Fawkes took his place on the scaffold. More penitent than any of his fellow conspirators, 'He beseeched all Catholics never to attempt such a bloody act, being a course which God did never favour or prosper.' Weak and still suffering from the appalling torture to which he had been subjected, he could hardly climb the ladder, 'yet with much ado, by the help of the hangman went high enough to break his neck with the fall.'

The other principal members of the conspiracy, Thomas Bates, Robert Winter, John Grant and Sir Everard Digby, were drawn on hurdles to the west end of St Paul's Churchyard and there hanged, drawn and quartered. It was reported by a spectator that when the executioner pulled out the heart of Everard Digby, held it high and shouted, 'Here is the heart of a traitor!' the 'dead' man exclaimed: 'Thou liest!'

The mutilated quarters of the eight Gunpowder Plotters were displayed over the gates of the city, and the spikes that flourished like a tropical forest on the Drawbridge Gate of London Bridge bore the eight heads as their hideous harvest; the bill, still in existence, shows that the amount paid for setting up the spikes was 23s 9d (£1.17p).

## FITZGERALD, THOMAS

In 1524 this gentleman's father, Gerald Fitzgerald, 9th Earl of Kildare, was Lord Justice and Lord Deputy of Ireland, tasked with controlling that turbulent country. He had many implacable enemies, one of whom, the Earl of Ossory, complained to Henry VIII that Kildare had invited Lord O'Neale and other Irish rebels to ravage his, Ossory's, estates. Fitzgerald was recalled to London for the matter to be investigated, leaving his son Thomas, Baron of Offaly, in charge. Other accusers, among them John Allen, Archbishop of Dublin, levelled similar charges of maladministration, and on arrival in England Gerald Fitzgerald was arrested and imprisoned in the Tower of London.

News of this quickly reached Ireland, as did rumours that the prisoner had been summarily tried and executed. At this his son Thomas, reputedly 'in matters of importance to be a headlong hotspur', reacted violently, renouncing his allegiance to the King, and, with five of his uncles, together with Lord O'Neale and others of the Irish nobility, went on the offensive by laying siege to Dublin Castle, the attackers identifying themselves by wearing silken fringes to their helmets (hence their leader's nickname 'Silken Thomas'). The siege of the Castle, defended by a small force commanded by Sir John White, was raised by the Earl of Ossory, but the rebels captured the Archbishop who, reportedly due to a misunderstanding, was killed by one of Thomas Fitzgerald's servants.

When word of this outrage reached the ears of Gerald Fitzgerald, incarcerated in the Tower, he died 'of a broken heart' on 12 December 1534 and was buried in the Royal Chapel of St Peter ad Vincula therein. Further retribution was then levied against Thomas and his allies, Henry VIII dispatching Sir William Skeffington with reinforcements to Ireland to suppress the rebellion. They promptly captured Maynooth Castle, one of the rebels' strongholds, and hanged its defenders. Thomas Fitzgerald, determined to avenge his father's death, wrote to the Pope, complaining of the King's defection from the Roman Catholic faith and volunteering to defend the kingdom of Ireland on behalf of His Holiness.

He withstood the King's forces until the middle of the

following year, 1535, but eventually a truce was arranged and he surrendered, together with his five uncles, to Lord Leonard Grey (ironically, his uncle by marriage, his sister having married Gerald Fitzgerald) who prevailed on them to travel to London under escort and submit to the King's mercy. On arrival at the quayside they were horrified to find that the ship in which they were due to sail to England was named *The Cow* for, according to an ancient Irish legend, it was prophesied that five sons of a certain earl would go to England in the belly of a cow and never return! On disembarking, Thomas and his five uncles, Sir James, Sir John, Oliver, Richard and Walter Fitzgerald, were interrogated by the Council and committed to the Tower. It then became only too apparent that not only was Henry's 'mercy' of a decidedly unreliable nature, but that they were indeed those men to whom the ancient legend referred – for on 3 February 1537 all were hanged, drawn and quartered.

## FRASER (or FREYSEL), SIR SIMON

Sir Simon Fraser was one of William Wallace's most renowned supporters. Indeed, his prowess on the battle-field was held in such high esteem that he was considered by his colleagues to be invincible, a stubborn belief which brought nothing but grief to those who staked their very lives on it, for he was captured at the Battle of Kyrkenclyf. What happened next is described in a chronicle compiled by Matthew of Westminster (the *nom de plume* of a group of St Albans and Westminster monks) and printed in 1567:

Simon Freysel was taken prisoner, a man in whom the whole confidence of the Scots was placed, insomuch that the Scotch nobles who were in prison asserted that he could not be subdued or taken; and while he was still alive, they thought the Scots could not be subdued.

And one certain Scotch knight who was in chains in the Tower of London gave the King leave to cut off his head if ever Simon Freysel was taken prisoner. His name was Herebert of Norham, the most beautiful in person and the tallest in stature of all the Scots. After capture Simon Freysel was sent to the Tower so that the other Scot (Herebert), on seeing him, would recollect the vow he had taken. On the morrow therefore, Herebert and Thomas de Boye, his esquire, were led out of the Tower and beheaded.

As for Simon Fraser, an ancient ballad narrates how, on 7 September 1306, he was taken from the Tower through Cheapside to Tyburn with a garland on his head and fetters on his legs, and when he 'com to Galewes, furst he wos an honge', then quickly beheaded, although to the victim 'him thohte it longe'. After that he was 'yopened, is boweles ybrend', his body being gibbetted for twenty days, then cut down and burnt. And the ballad relates how his head 'to London brugge wos send', where many wives and children who saw the skull close beside that of Wallace said, 'Alas! that he wes ibore.'

# GAVESTON, PIERS, EARL OF CORNWALL

The coronation of Edward II in 1307 was almost a total shambles and Piers Gaveston, the foster brother and favourite of the King, was the man responsible for organizing both the ceremony and the banquet which followed. Thanks to his inefficiency, it was three o'clock before the consecration of the royal couple was over and the short wintry days protracted the banquet till dark. This lateness made the hungry nobles even more furious than any of Gaveston's misdeeds that day; the food was badly cooked and ill served, with a total lack of ceremony, and the Queen went to the lengths of complaining to her father, the King of France, about Gaveston's attitude and behaviour.

Although the favourite had been given the title of Earl of Cornwall on Edward's accession to the throne, such was the debacle of the coronation feast that, at the insistence of the barons, Gaveston was banished from the country. By the following year, however, he had been appointed Lieutenant of Ireland and, on returning to court in 1308 continued to offend his fellow peers with his arrogant manner and spendthift ways. He was resented particularly for his abusive taunts, derisively referring to the Earl of Lancaster as 'the play actor', the Earl of Warwick as 'the black dog of Arden' and the Earl of Pembroke as 'Joseph the Jew'.

Eventually, in 1311 he was again banished by the barons who had by then taken over the King's affairs; but he returned secretly, spending Christmas Day with Edward at Windsor and later accompanying him to Yorkshire where Edward was fighting the barons, led by the Earl of Lancaster, in order to regain control of the kingdom. There, Gaveston was captured in Scarborough Castle and surrendered to the Earl of Pembroke, being granted a safe conduct. But one of his old enemies, Warwick, kidnapped him and his subsequent arrival at his enemy's camp in Kenilworth on a mule was greeted with mock honours and much derision.

On 19 June 1312, protesting desperately for mercy, he was hustled to Blacklow Hill where, with the Earls of Lancaster, Hereford and Surrey as vengeful onlookers, he was forced to his knees by a common soldier who then drew his sword – and the head of Piers Gaveston, Earl of Cornwall, rolled in the dust by the roadside.

# GENINGS, EDMUND

In Elizabethan times the presence in England of Roman Catholic priests practising their religion was contrary to the law and anyone found sheltering them could expect little mercy from the courts. Even those members of a family unaware of sanctuary having been given to a priest were equally liable to condign punishment, as Mr Swithin Wels found out to his cost when in December 1591, he returned from work to his home in London – to discover that not only was his house locked and barred but his wife was in Newgate Prison! He immediately approached a local judge, Justice Yonge by name, and requested that his wife be freed and his house keys returned to him, on the grounds that he had not been aware of any goings-on in his house. The dignitary informed him that a fugitive priest had been discovered there and, according to the historian Stow: 'The Justice then told him in playne termes, he came time inough to taste of the sauce, although he were ignorant how the meate savoured,' and promptly sent him to join his wife in Newgate.

The fate of Mrs Wels is not recorded, though doubtless the 'taste of the sauce' she was given was hardly of a palatable nature. What is known, however, is that on 10 December of that year her husband was hanged in Grays Inn Field, where the priest, Edmund Genings, also suffered, Stow relating how:

> He being ripped up & his bowelles cast into the fire, if credit may be giuen to hundreds of People standing by, and to the Hangman himselfe [probably Bull, the executioner who dispatched Mary, Queen of Scots with such marked inaccuracy] the blessed Martyr uttered – his hart being in the Executioners hand – these words, *Sancte Gregori ora pro me!* Which the Hangman hearing, with open mouth

swore this damnable oath; Gods woundes, See his hart is in my hand and yet Gregori is in his mouth; o egregious Papist!

# GRAHAM, JAMES, EARL OF MONTROSE

Vilified by many Scots for the backing he gave to the English King, Charles I, loathed by his bitter rivals the Argylls, nevertheless James Graham bore a charmed, if brutally terminated life, being executed at the age of thirty-eight. In 1641 he supported Charles I but was imprisoned by the Earl of Argyll, later being freed by the King. However, when that monarch was captured by the Parliamentary forces, Montrose escaped to the Continent, where he was made field-marshal by Emperor Ferdinand III and granted permission to raise a Royalist army. On 12 April 1650 he landed in Caithness and, having lost many of his men in a shipwreck and failing to receive the military support he expected, he was defeated at Carbisdaile. On the run, he appealed to his friend Neil McLeod of Assynt to help him escape capture, but instead McLeod handed him over to his foes for the reward of four hundred bolls of meal. McLeod paid dearly for his treachery, for not only did he fail to receive his ill-deserved reward but some time later his castle was burnt almost to the ground, only ruins surviving to this day.

Montrose was led ignominiously through the length of the country to Edinburgh, an eyewitness describing how:

He still wore the peasant's clothes in which he had been caught, with a ragged old reddish plaid around his shoulders, seated upon a little shelty horse without a saddle but on a quilt of sacks and straw, with lengths of rope for stirrups. His ankles were tied under the horse's belly with a tether and, his wounds having been neglected, he was in a high fever. In front of his poor mount strode a herald who relished his task of proclaiming 'Here comes James Graham, a traitor to his country!'

On arrival at Edinburgh's Canongate he was met by the executioner, who transferred his prisoner to a waiting cart in which he had to sit tied in a chair with his back to the horse. This conveyance, led by the executioner and preceded by a number of his fellow prisoners bound together in pairs, wended its way along Edinburgh's main street to the prison where he would await trial. On its route the grim procession reached Moray House in which, coincidentally, festivities were taking place to celebrate the marriage of Lord Lorn, the eldest son of Montrose's bitter enemy, the Earl of Argyll, to Lady Mary Stewart, daughter of the Earl of Moray. To gratify the wedding party, the cart stopped for a few minutes and it was reported that one of the bridal guests who were standing on the balcony and at the windows, Lady Jane Gordon, Countess of Haddington, actually spat at Montrose! The Argylls themselves indulged in a little sadistic gloating, the Marchioness of Argyll making no effort to conceal her hatred of the doomed prisoner, unaware that a few years hence her husband, Archibald, the 'glae-eyed Marquis', would take the same journey, his head replacing Montrose's on public display.

At the gaol the cart stopped and as the executioner released his prisoner from the chair and helped him down, Montrose tipped him with a coin and thanked him for having driven his chariot so well! After the hearing in court, he was forced to kneel as the dread sentence was read out, the *Notes of Parliament* stating that:

He was to be hanged on a gibbet at the Cross of Edinburgh with the declaration of his crime tied on a rope  ·

about his neck and there to be hanged for the space of three hours until he be dead, and thereafter to be cut down by the hangman, his head, hands and legs to be cut off and distributed as follows; viz. his head to be fixed on an iron pin and set on the pinnacle of the west gavel of the new prison of Edinburgh: one hand to be set on the port [gate] of Perth, the other on the port of Stirling: one leg and foot on the port of Aberdeen, the other on the port of Glasgow. If at his death penitent and relaxed from excommunication [i.e. not excommunicated], then the trunk of his body to be interred in the Greyfriars, otherwise to be interred by the hangman under the gallows.

Loyal to the end, Montrose defiantly replied that he was much indebted to Parliament for the great honour they had decreed him, and that he was prouder to have his head placed on top of the prison than if they had decreed a golden statue to be erected to him in the market place or that his picture should be hung in the King's bedchamber. He also thanked them for their care to preserve the remembrance of his loyalty by transmitting such monuments (i.e. the parts of his dismembered body) to the different parts of the kingdom and only wished that he had flesh enough to have sent a piece to every city in Christendom as a token of his unshaken fidelity to his King and country.

At 3 pm on the following morning, 21 May 1650, dressed in clothes brought in by friends, a black suit with a richly laced scarlet cloak, a black beaver hat with a silver band and wearing stockings of carnation silk, he was paraded through the streets to the Cross, there to mount the scaffold, above which towered the thirty-foot-high gallows. After a brief prayer he allowed the executioner to pinion his arms and then ascended the ladder. 'God have mercy on this afflicted land!' he exclaimed as the ladder was turned. His gyrating body was quickly cut down and, laying it out on the bench, the executioner swiftly severed the head, then held it high, proclaiming, 'Behold the head of a traitor!' as he did so. The ghastly process of quartering the torso followed, the mutilated parts to be exhibited in the other Scottish cities, the parboiled head later being spiked on the Tolbooth roof from where it would stare blindly across the city for the next eleven years.

## GREY, LADY JANE

On the death of Henry VIII in 1547, his ten-year-old son, a weak and ailing child, became Edward VI. The young King was strongly influenced by John Dudley, Duke of Northumberland, who persuaded him that since his sisters, Mary and Elizabeth, were ineligible for variously contrived legal reasons to succeed to the throne, he should, in the event of his death, be followed by his second cousin, Lady Jane Grey, a great-granddaughter of Henry VII. Having achieved this, Northumberland promptly had his son Guildford marry Jane, calculating that should the King soon die, as seemed likely, his daughter-in-law would be Queen and even if his son did not actually become King, at least his own personal position would be one of immeasurable power in the country.

When Edward VI did die, at the age of sixteen, Northumberland proclaimed Jane Queen of England and she entered the Royal Palace of the Tower of London 'with a grett company of lords and nobulls, and there was a shott of gunne and chambers as has nott been seen oft.' The public, however, knowing little about her and probably seeing through the ruse employed by Northumberland, backed Mary to succeed to the throne. And when Northumberland marched north from London with ten thousand or so supporters, intent on rallying the country and capturing Mary, who by then had the almost total support of the eastern counties, the people showed their feelings by a stubborn silence. 'The people crowd to look upon us,' the Duke noted gloomily, 'but not one calls, God spede ye.' As the days passed, even his own followers started to fall away, until at length Northumberland realized that all was lost; at Cambridge, knowing that the game was up, he threw his cap in the air and shouted with those men still with him, for Queen Mary. His change of heart, however, did not help him; arrested, he was imprisoned in the Tower and later, although he vowed himself to be a Roman Catholic in an attempt to save his neck, the axe nevertheless descended on it.

Jane's status as Queen, a role she had neither desired nor sought, ended after nine days when, on 19 July 1553, Mary was proclaimed Queen. Jane remained in the Tower but as a prisoner, together with her husband, Guildford. Four months later, on 12 November, both were brought to trial charged with high treason for 'having levied war against the Queen and conspiring to set up another in her room (place).' Both pleaded guilty, and Jane was sentenced 'to be burnt alive on Tower Hill or beheaded as the Queen pleases'. There seems little doubt that Mary was inclined to show mercy to the young couple, if not to the Duke who had so cunningly manipulated them, but all hope of clemency vanished when Jane's father, Henry, Duke of Suffolk, joined in an insurrection raised by Sir Thomas Wyatt. In those times, whenever the throne was threatened, the solution was to remove the rivals permanently, and this certainly held good in 1553.

Because the government was concerned about the deleterious effect the spectacle of the seventeen-year-old Jane and her husband being so savagely executed together in public on Tower Hill might have on the people, it was decided to separate the venues; Guildford would be dispatched on the Hill and Jane on Tower Green within the battlements. And so at ten o'clock on the cold and misty morning of 12 February 1554 the young man was taken to the scaffold and there beheaded, after which: 'His carcas throwne into a carre and his hed in a cloth, he was brought back into the Tower, wher the Lady Jane dyd see his ded carcase taken out of the cart, as well as she dyd see hym before alyve going to deathe, a syght to hir no less than deathe . . .'

By that time the scaffold had been erected on the Green, to which she was led by her weeping ladies-in-waiting, Mistress Elisabeth Tylney and Mistress Eleyn. Wearing a black gown, a cap lined and edged with velvet and a black French hood, she mounted the scaffold and, facing those assembled on the Green, she admitted the unlawfulness of her act against the Queen but protested before God her innocence of intention. After she had said a psalm with her chaplain, the hooded and masked executioner attempted to help her remove her gown, but:

she desyred him to let her alone, turning towards her two gentlewomen who helped her off therwith, and also her neckercher and frose paste [a matronly headdress, the words later evolving into 'frow's piece' and eventually to 'frontispiece' as at the front of a book], geving to her a fayre handkercher to knytte about her eyes. Then the hangman kneled downe and asked forgevenes whom she forgave most willingly. Then he willed her to stand upon the straw, which doing she sawe the blocke. Then she sayd, 'I pray you despatche me quickly.' Then she kneeled downe saying, 'Will you take it of before I lay me downe?' and the hangman answered her, 'No, Madame.'

She tied the kercher about her eyes. Then feeling for the block, saide, 'What shal I do? Where is it?' One of the standers-by guyding her therunto, she layde her head downe upon the block and stretched forth her body and said, 'Lord into Thy handes I commende my spirite,' and so she ended.

Her remains were placed in a coffin and carried the few yards into the Royal Chapel of St Peter ad Vincula, there to be buried without any religious rites, between those of the other two English Queens to have similarly suffered, Anne Boleyn and Katherine Howard, albeit for very different reasons.

As a token of appreciation for the small kindnesses Sir John Bridges, the Lieutenant of the Tower, had shown her, Jane gave him a manual of devotions in which she had written a few words of thanks, adding, 'For as the precher sayethe, there is a tyme to be born and a tyme to die; and the daye of deathe is better than the daye of our birthe' and signing herself: 'Youres, as the Lorde knowethe, as a frende, Jane Duddeleye'. A brave lady who met a tragic and undeserved end.

## GREY, HENRY, DUKE OF SUFFOLK

Henry Grey, Duke of Suffolk, 3rd Marquis of Dorset and Privy Councillor, was the father of Lady Jane Grey, but he relinquished her claim to the throne and supported Mary's right to rule. Later, however, he rashly supported Sir Thomas Wyatt in an uprising against the Queen's intention to marry Philip of Spain. Leading a group of about a hundred supporters in an attempt to seize Coventry on Tuesday, 30 January 1553/4, he had no alternative but to abort the effort when he found the city gates barred against him and the inhabitants unwilling to join him, so he shared what little money he had with his men and advised them to scatter and avoid capture. He himself made his way to Astley Park and there hid in the hollow of a tree, but the bitter cold and rain forced him to abandon his shelter and seek refuge in a nearby cottage.

However, the hunt was up, for a manservant of his named Underwood betrayed him and, 'most dusty and shabby with his cloak in tatters and his cap lost', he was brought to London with an escort of three hundred horsemen.

He was condemned to death for high treason and, a few days after his daughter's execution on 12 February 1554, he was escorted to the public execution site on Tower Hill, there to mount the scaffold steps. Although he was accompanied by Dr Weston, the Queen's Chaplain, he sought to dispense with the cleric's spiritual comfort by pushing the Dean aside and climbing the steps with his arms outspread, but eventually permitted the cleric to join him in prayers. Afterwards he removed his gown and doublet, cap and scarf, and as was the custom, presented them to the waiting executioner who, kneeling, begged his forgiveness. 'God forgive thee, and I doo,' said the Duke, as quoted by a contemporary historian. 'And when thou doest thine office, I praie thee doo it quicklie, and God have mercie to thee.' The executioner, nervous or simply incompetent, took two strokes with the axe to remove the Duke's head, which he then held high so all could see that the right man had indeed been executed.

The head was taken away but was later retrieved, either from the coffin or from display on London Bridge, and subsequently buried in the vault of the family's chapel, their mansion being situated in what is now a street called the Minories near the Tower of London. As the decades passed, the area was redeveloped, the chapel and house being demolished and replaced by the Church of the Holy Trinity, and in 1852 the head was discovered by Lord Dartmouth in a small vault near the altar. As recorded by the Rev Samuel Kinnes in his extensively entitled book, *Six Hundred Years of Historical Sketches of Eminent Men and Women who have more or less come into contact with the Abbey and Church of Holy Trinity, Minories, from 1293–1893*, published in 1898:

He came across something that might have been a basket full of sawdust, but on examining it he found it to contain a head in a remarkable state of preservation. I think it most probable that it was oaken sawdust which, acting as an antiseptic, had not only preserved the head from decay, but had so mummified it that the features have remained sufficiently perfect for anyone acquainted with the Duke's likeness to recognize him, and indeed, the late Sir George Scharf, Keeper of the National Portrait Gallery, thought he found the features to agree well with those of the Duke in *Lodge's Portraits*. I think it possible that if the sawdust was that of oak, it would really tan the skin of the face to leather in the most natural way imaginable. The hair of the head came away with the sawdust and the basket had quite perished.

The head was later examined by a surgical expert, Mr Mouat, who assessed it as:

belonging to a man past the prime of life, and that the head was removed by rapid decapitation during life admits of no doubt. A large gaping gash, which had not divided the subcutaneous structures, shows that the first stroke of the axe was misdirected too near the occiput, and in a slanting direction. The retraction of the skin, the violent, convulsive action of the muscles, and the formation of a cup-like cavity with the body of the spinal bone at the base, prove that the severance was effected during life and in cold weather.

The Church ceased to be a place of worship in 1899 and, despite a bid being made by an American gentleman who offered £500 for the relic, it was transferred to the nearby St Botolph's Church, Aldgate where, earlier this century, the vicar would give the morbidly curious permission to view the mummified head in its airtight glass container. One visitor who surveyed it, purely for academic reasons, was Sir George Younghusband who afterwards described it in some detail:

> There is no shrinkage of the face, the eyes are wide open and the eyeballs and pupils perfectly preserved, though of a parchment colour. The skin too, all over is of the same yellowish hue. When found, the hair of the head and beard were still on, but owing to its very brittle state and from being handled by several people, these broke off, though in a strong light the bristles may still be seen. The nose is not quite perfect, but the ears are practically as in life. The head had evidently been severed by two heavy blows, and loose skin, jagged and looking like loose parchment, demonstrates where the severance occurred.

Some half century or more later, respect for the grim relic was finally shown, and it was interred in the consecrated ground beneath the paving stones at the church's entrance – a mere arrow's flight from where the pitiful remains of his daughter, Lady Jane Grey, lie buried within the Tower of London.


# HALL, JOHN

In the late 1300s England was in the grip of social revolution due to exorbitant taxes and weak government. The King, Richard II, was facing strong opposition from a powerful group led by two men, the Earl of Arundel and the King's uncle, Thomas of Woodstock, Earl of Buckingham, Duke of Gloucester. The latter knight, the seventh and youngest son of Edward III, had not only played a major role in repelling a

French invasion at Dover in 1380 but had also captured eight Spanish ships off Brest. After years of sometimes violent unrest in their efforts to unseat the King, defeat came in July 1397 when Arundel was arrested and executed. Government forces attacked and overran Gloucester's magnificently constructed castle at Pleshey, near Chelmsford in Essex, the Duke himself being captured. Some indication of the owner's affluence and lifestyle was revealed when, the contents being confiscated by the King, the inventory was found to include 'a great bed of gold'!

To deprive his supporters of their leader, Gloucester was taken under strong guard to France and imprisoned in Calais, an English possession at that time. Within a matter of weeks he had died, his death being officially attributed to a fit of apoplexy but it was more likely to have been murder initiated by Richard's intention to rid himself of an uncle who constantly opposed him and even threatened to depose him. Indeed, rumours abounded that four knights had crossed the Channel with orders either to strangle or smother the recalcitrant Duke, although no one was accused of complicity until two years later. Then, as related by Kingsford in his *Chronicles of London*:

One John Hall was charged with having kept the door of the room when the Duke was done to death by being smothered in a feather bed. And on 17 October 1399 'the lordes were examyned what peyne the same John Halle hadde desyrved ffor his knowyng off the deeth off the Duk off Gloustre; and the lordes seyden, that he were worthy off the moste grete peyne and penaunce that he myght have. And so the Juggement was that the same John Halle shulde be drawe ffro the Tour off London to Tyborne and there his bowelles shulde be brent [burnt] and affterwarde he shulde be hangid and quarterid and byhedid.

And his heede y-brouht to the same place wher the Duk
off Gloucestre was murdred.

The historian Froussart in his *Chronicles of England, France
and Spain* told how, following Richard's later abdication in
favour of Henry IV, four knights were indeed arrested, Sir
Bernard Brocas, Lord Marclais, John Derby, Receiver of
Lincoln, and Lord Stelle, Steward of the King's Household.
After being first paraded in the Tower in full view of the apart-
ment in which Richard was confined, they were then dragged
on sledges by horses through the crowded streets to Cheapside
and, on a fishmonger's stall, were decapitated, their heads
displayed on London Bridge and their bodies hung on a gibbet.
Froissart concludes his narrative by adding: 'After this execution every man returned to his home'. Except, of course,
Messrs Brocas, Marclais, Derby and Stelle!

Richard II was later transferred to Pontefract Castle in
Yorkshire where, on 14 February 1400, he met a violent death
– alas too late for poor John Hall's possible acquittal on the
grounds of being an unwilling accomplice to the Duke of
Gloucester's murder.

# HAMILTON, JOHN

A native of the county of Clydesdale in Scotland, John
Hamilton was related to the ducal family of the same
name. His parents, wishing the best for their only son, sent
him to study law at Glasgow, but he had other ideas, preferring
instead to apply for a commission in the army. However, his
ambition in this respect was sadly thwarted when, having
been duped into joining some profligate gentlemen at the card
tables in Edinburgh, he lost a considerable amount of money.
Pleas to his parents resulted in some slight relief to his cash

flow problems but this was accompanied by warnings that there would be no further financial help.

On receipt of the money, he joined his fellow gamblers again, this time at an inn situated in a small village near Glasgow, mine host being one Thomas Arkle. There the sessions continued day and night with hardly a break until Hamilton decided to get some sleep, and while he was doing so, his companions fled, leaving him to settle the substantial account they owed. Hamilton, bereft of the wherewithal, was accused by the innkeeper of being a swindling scoundrel, this inevitably developing into a fierce argument and Hamilton decided to avoid further trouble by removing himself from the premises as quickly as possible. At that, Arkle, in attempting to stop Hamilton from escaping, grappled with him but only succeeded in depriving him of his sword scabbard. All would have been well had not Hamilton, on realizing his loss, turned back and re-entered the inn. On doing so he was greeted by a torrent of doubtlessly justified abuse and, drawing his sword from his belt, he stabbed the innkeeper to death.

Unfortunately for Hamilton, Thomas Arkle's daughter was present and although almost blind, nevertheless attempted to defend her father. In the struggle that ensued she managed to tear the skirt from his coat and that evidence, together with the sword which still protruded from her father's chest, was handed over to the authorities. But the bird had flown, Hamilton making his way to Leith and at that port boarding a ship bound for Holland. There he took refuge for two years until, on his parents' death, he returned in order to benefit from the estate, but the officers of the law had not forgotten him and he was taken into custody and put on trial. In his defence he pleaded that he had been drunk and also provoked by his victim's aggressive attitude, but to no avail; he was found guilty of murder and sentenced to death.

The loss suffered by the fatherless Scottish lass was atoned for to some degree on 30 June 1716 in Edinburgh's Grassmarket, when other innkeepers did a roaring trade in catering for the needs of the thirsty thousands who assembled to watch as John Hamilton, gambler and murderer, knelt before another Scottish Maiden and lost, not his scabbard, but his head.

# HARCLA, ANDREW of, EARL OF CARLISLE

The blame for the defeat of the English by the Scots at the Abbey of Byland on 14 October 1322 fell on Andrew de Harcla for keeping his two thousand foot and mounted soldiers out of the battle and, after his collusion with the enemy had been proved, a writ signed by Edward II at Knaresborough, Yorkshire, on 27 February 1323 declared:

> that he should be stripped of his Earl's robes and ensigns of knighthood, his sword broken over his head, his gilt spurs hacked from his heels and that he should be drawn to the place of execution and there hanged by the neck; his heart, from whence cometh his treacherous thoughts, together with his bowels, be taken out of his body, burnt to ashes and winnowed, his body cut into four quarters, one to be set up on the principal tower of Carlisle Castle, another on the tower of Newcastle on Tyne, a third on the bridge of York, the fourth at Shrewsbury, and his head on London Bridge.

De Harcla's sister later petitioned Edward III for restitution of the remains for burial and His Majesty mercifully issued this order:

> The King, to his faithful and beloved Warden of Carlisle Castle, greetings. We command that you cause to be deliv-

ered without delay the quarter of the body of Andrew de Harcla, which hangs by the command of the Lord Edward, late King of England, our father, upon the walls of the said Castle, to our beloved Sarah, sister of the aforesaid Andrew, to whom we of our grace have granted that she may collect together the bones of the same Andrew and commit them to holy sepulchre whenever she wishes. And this you shall in no wise omit. Witness the King at York, 10 August 1337.

Although no traces of the Earl's family residence remain in the hamlet of Hartley (originally Harcla), the portions of the body so retrieved were later buried in the de Harcla tomb in the ancient church of the nearby village, Kirkby Stephen, Cumbria, where large marrowless bones were discovered interred there in 1847, the burial of the remains being commemorated by a brass plate on an inner wall.

## HARRISON, THOMAS, MAJOR-GENERAL

Anyone considering bringing about the death of a monarch should first take note of the ghastly fate suffered by Thomas Harrison, one of those who passed sentence of death on Charles I. Upon the accession of Charles II to the throne, he and many other regicides were rounded up and put on trial. The result was a foregone conclusion, little time being wasted before the Judge passed sentence on the prisoner, declaring that 'your private parts be cut off, and your bowels within your belly be taken and put upon a fire and burned while you live, and your head be cut off, and your body be divided into four parts to be placed where it may please His Majesty the King to assign them.' And so, as described in a contemporary broadsheet:

On Saturday, 13 October 1660, betwixt nine and ten of the clock in the morning, Major-General Thomas Harrison was upon a hurdle drawn from Newgate Gaol to the place called Charing Cross, where within certain rails lately there made, a gibbet was erected, and he hanged with his face looking towards the Banqueting House at Whitehall, the place where our late Sovereign of Eternal memory was sacrificed; being half-dead, he was cut down by the common executioner, his privy members cut off before his eyes, his bowels burned, his head severed from his body and his body divided into quarters, which were returned to Newgate upon the same hurdle that carried it. His head is since set on a pole on the top of the south-east end of Westminster Hall looking towards London. The quarters of his body are in a like manner exposed upon some of the city gates.

The hangman, believed to be one 'Squire' Edward Dun, an executioner infamous for his brutal habit of taunting his victims, was no doubt taken aback when, while he was busy disembowelling his half-strangled victim, Harrison reportedly leant forward and struck his tormentor a violent blow! His head was indeed returned to Newgate but not for the immediate purpose of parboiling prior to display; instead it was affixed to the hurdle conveying the next victim, John Cooke, ex-Solicitor General of the Commonwealth, who had actually conducted Charles I's trial. Cooke therefore had the added horror of having his friend's severed head nodding and swaying in front of him during his own journey to the scaffold.

Ironically Harrison's republican principles did not die with him. One of his sons escaped to Virginia where he settled and raised a family, a grandson being one of those who signed the Declaration of Independence. That grandson had a boy who later joined the army and, as General William Henry

Harrison, fought against the English in 1812 and in turn *his* grandson, Benjamin, also became a general – who in 1891 was elected the twenty-third President of the United States of America.

# HINDE, CAPTAIN JAMES

The advent of Cromwell's Commonwealth in the mid-1600s did little to reduce the amount of crime, the highwaymen, cutpurses, footpads and the like taking little notice of the change in politics. When captured, they usually provided the public with entertainment by first being hanged, following which their tar-coated cadavers served as macabre warnings by being suspended from gibbets erected at busy crossroads. But one particular gentleman of the road might possibly have earned inclusion in the Underworld Book of Records' category of 'the only highwayman to be hanged, drawn and quartered', a distinction he could no doubt well have done without.

He was James Hinde, born in 1618 at Chipping Norton in Oxfordshire, the only son of a saddler who, after providing him with a good education, apprenticed him to a local butcher. After two years or so of boning and slicing, he realized that this was not the career for him and so, borrowing some money from his mother, he departed to find his fortune in London. There, while partaking of pleasures not usually available in his home village with a young lady he had happened to meet on the street, he was arrested, his fair companion being accused of stealing five guineas from the pocket of an old gentleman. James spent the night in the Poultry Compter, the temporary gaol of the watch, but was released the next morning for want of evidence. However, a fellow inmate happened to be Thomas Allen, a notorious highwayman, with whom James struck up an instant rapport and as his new friend was also released at the same time, James decided that his future lay with joining Allen in partnership as a gentleman of the road.

It was about this time that Charles I was beheaded, an event which, in 1649, resulted in the public taking up even more partisan attitudes than before. James came from a county in which the late King had made his headquarters during the Civil War and he was a keen upholder of the Stuart cause. Allen felt likewise and so the duo swore to make life particularly hard for any regicide passengers aboard stage-coaches they happened to waylay. However, some months later, while holding up and robbing a coach on the Great North Road, they nearly received more than they had bargained for. Having halted the vehicle, Allen covered the driver with his flintlock while James was inviting the passengers to contribute to his personal savings account when, suddenly, the sound of an approaching troop of horsemen caused them to abandon their operation. This was no ordinary party of horse-men but Oliver Cromwell himself with his escort. After a chase, Allen was captured, three of the escort taking up pursuit of James who, luckily having the better mount, succeeded in escaping. His fellow highwayman, however, was not so lucky and received short shrift and a shorter rope, his corpse later swinging from the Caxton gibbet.

James Hinde now set up in business on his own, adopting the rank of captain and, recruiting a gang of twenty or more highwaymen, operating right across the Midlands. Although he was a dangerous man to defy, nevertheless he relied on his menacing appearance and his pistol to force his victims into handing over their valuables, never using violence towards them. It was bitterly ironic therefore that his eventual capture resulted from the only occasion on which he did so.

He had committed a number of robberies in the woods surrounding Maidenhead, so many in fact that the authorities had set up an intensive network of patrols in the area and, on being warned of this by a friendly innkeeper, he decided to seek fresh fields until the pressure was off. Accordingly, he left his gang and set out, but as he approached Knole Hill, not far from Maidenhead, he heard the sounds of a horse coming along the track behind him. Fearing it was a pursuer, one moreover on a fresher mount than his own and closing fast, he pulled out his pistol, turned in the saddle and fired. On seeing the man fall, James galloped on and reached London where, to avoid capture, he adopted the name of Brown and joined those fighting on behalf of Prince Charles. When the Royalists were defeated at the Battle of Worcester on 3 September 1651 he managed to escape capture and made his way back to London, finding lodgings with a Mr Denzie who had a barber's shop in Fleet Street. But as evidence that the glib phrase 'honour among thieves' was a complete fallacy, he was recognized by a so-called friend who decided that being given cash in hand was preferable to giving a friendly hand, and so denounced his comrade and claimed the reward offered by the authorities.

Hinde was taken before the Speaker of the House of Commons who lived nearby in Chancery Lane, and was then committed to Newgate Gaol, there to be put in irons. On 12 December 1651 he stood trial at the Old Bailey but when charges alleging his career as a highwayman could not be substantiated, he was held in gaol until March 1651/2 when he was taken to Reading and there charged with murdering one George Sympson who, far from wishing him harm, had not even been aware of James's identity but had been simply trying to catch up with his master who had ridden on ahead of him.

Although found guilty, James assumed a reprieve would be granted, for Parliament had recently issued an amnesty for all prisoners whose offences were not against the State. But it was not to be, for the new charge levelled against him was that he had fought for the King against the Commonwealth, and so he was arraigned for treason. The trial was short-lived, as was the prisoner, for he was sentenced to be hanged, drawn and quartered, and on 24 September 1652, at the age of thirty-four, the self-styled Captain James Hinde was taken to Worcester's scaffold. There he faced the crowds of morbid spectators to declare that most of his robberies were committed against leading members of the Parliamentary party, that he was a true Royalist and that his one regret was that he was to die before he saw his royal master take his rightful place on the throne.

The hangman allowed him to complete his speech, then duly turned him off the ladder, after which he proceeded to disembowel, decapitate, then quarter him. The latter remains were spiked atop the city's gates and his head displayed on the Bridge Gate over the River Severn – from where, reportedly, a week later, some sympathetic person of doubtless Royalist tendencies removed it and gave it a Christian burial.

# HOTHAM, SIR JOHN
# HOTHAM, CAPTAIN JOHN

Perhaps the fact that Sir John married five times and his son, also named John, followed his father's example on three occasions, was indicative of their inability to make the correct decisions when it really mattered, a family trait which proved fatal to both of them.

Sir John, a proud Yorkshireman, was created baronet in 1622 and soon after became Sheriff of his home county and Member of Parliament for Beverley. In the political turmoil of the 1640s between Charles I and Parliament, Sir John professed his allegiance to Cromwell and, early in April 1642, was sent as Governor to Hull, which at that time contained vast stores of weapons and ammunitions, in order to deny their use by the Royalists. However, Charles, based in York, believed that as King, he had every right to those armaments. Accordingly on 23 April 1642 he, together with two or three hundred servants and gentry of the country, rode towards the town, sending a messenger on ahead to Sir John announcing that he, the King, would dine with him that day. But the royal fury was doubtless much in evidence when, on approaching Hull 'he found the gates shut, the bridges up, the walls manned, and all things ready as for the reception of an enemy.'

Sir John appeared on the walls and in an agitated manner explained that he dare not admit the King in defiance of Parliamentary orders. Charles then proposed that he enter with just twenty horsemen as escort; this was also rejected by the Governor, as was the offer that if Sir John would come out and discuss the situation, he would be given safe conduct to return behind the walls. Despite Sir John's apologetic attitude, the King immediately proclaimed him a traitor and returned with his entourage to Beverley.

By the following year Sir John, either genuinely despairing of the state of the country brought about by the Civil War which was then raging, or deciding to back the side he concluded would eventually win, agreed to negotiate with Charles if a secret meeting could be arranged with a suitable envoy. Accordingly, one such gentleman, Lord Digby, smuggled himself into Hull aboard a ship and when arrested, pretended to be a Frenchman and in broken English made his guard understand that 'if he could speak privately to the governor, he would disclose some secrets of the King's which would highly advance the service of the Parliament.' Then, identifying himself to Sir John, Lord Digby painted a glowing picture of the rewards available to anyone who would thus assist the royal cause: riches, title and incalculable glory. Whereupon Sir

John offered to surrender Hull if the King should return with a force large enough to give him the excuse to do so.

But, unfortunately for the baronet, new officers arrived from London to assist in defending the town, and somehow the plot was uncovered. Sir John was accused of high treason and in December 1644 was condemned to death by court martial, for 'betraying his trust and adhering to the enemy; for refusing to supply Lord Fairfax [a Roundhead General] with ammunition; for scandalous words against the Parliament; for endeavouring to betray Hull to the King; for corresponding with the Queen and for seeking to make his escape.'

Meanwhile, Sir John's son had embarked with vigour in the Parliamentary cause and in 1640 became Member of Parliament for Scarborough. With the rank of captain, he fought against the Royalists at Tadcaster and Sherburn, but three years later, suspected of treachery, he was imprisoned at Nottingham. A resourceful and daring man, he escaped and, making his way to the Continent, conspired with the Queen then in exile in France. Returning to England, he made contact with the royalist Marquis of Newcastle, but he was betrayed by a servant and arrested at about the same time as was his father. The outcome was inevitable. He was tried at the Guildhall by a council of war, found guilty of high treason and sentenced to death.

It was ordered that both men should be beheaded by the axe on Tower Hill, Sir John on New Year's Eve 1644, his son on the following day, and the crowds of spectators massing at the execution site on 31 December watched with excited anticipation as Sir John was led from the Tower to where the scaffold, coffin and executioner waited in readiness. One can therefore appreciate their understandable disappointment, to put it mildly, when an order suddenly arrived from the House of Lords for a postponement and they saw the small procession turn about and march the condemned man back across the drawbridge.

On being later informed of the arbitrary action taken by the Lords, the Commons quickly asserted their authority and decreed that the executions would take place without further delay. So those Londoners of a bloodthirsty inclination were not deprived of their entertainment after all, the highlight of New Year's Day being the spectacle of Captain John Hotham's execution, the crowds reassembling the following day to watch his father, Sir John, mount the scaffold where, it was reported 'his execution was a most shocking scene; his spirits were greatly broken and in a state of utter desperation he committed his neck to the block.'

## HOUGHTON, FATHER JOHN

In the year 1535, during the reign of Henry VIII, proceedings were taken against the London Carthusians, members of a Roman Catholic religious Order, for failing to admit Henry's claim to be supreme head of the Church. Among the number brought to trial was the Prior of the Charterhouse, Father John Houghton, and all were condemned to death. On 4 May 1535, as recounted by Father Maurice Chauncy in his book *History of Some English Carthusian Martyrs*:

Being brought out of prison Father Houghton was thrown down on a hurdle and fastened to it, lying at length on his back and dragged at the heels of horses through the city until they came to Tyburn. On arrival at that place of execution our holy Father was first loosed and then, as the custom is, the executioner bent his knee before him, asking pardon for the cruel work he had to do, whereupon the Father embraced him and then prayed for him and all the bystanders. Then on being ordered to mount the ladder where he was to be hanged, he meekly obeyed.

The crowd gathered about the scaffold included the Dukes of Norfolk and Richmond, together with other members of the court, and while Father Houghton was on the ladder one of the King's Council approached him and promised him a pardon if he would submit to the King's command and abide by the Act of Parliament, but the Father replied that he was there, not through any malice or disobedience towards the King, but solely through fear of God. Chauncy's account continued:

> On a sign being given the ladder was turned and so he was hanged. Then one of the bystanders, before his holy soul had left his body, cut the coarse and heavy rope, and so falling to the ground he began for a little space to throb and breathe. Then he was drawn to another adjoining place where all his garments were violently torn off and he was again extended naked on the hurdle, on whom immediately the bloody executioner laid his wicked hands. In the first place he cut off his genitals, then he cut open his belly, dragged out his bowels, his heart and all else, and threw them into a fire, during which our most blessed Father not only did not cry out on account of the intolerable pain but on the contrary, during all this time until his heart was torn out, prayed continually. Lastly his head was cut off and the beheaded body was divided into four quarters.

The remains were thrown into cauldrons and parboiled, afterwards being put up in various places in the city, with the exception of the left arm which was nailed above the gate of the Charterhouse as a hideous reminder to the monks of the fate that had befallen their superior. One day it fell down at the feet of two of them, Thomas Monday and Thurstan Hickman, and was quickly hidden. Contacting two other monks who had previously escaped to the Continent, they promised to bring the severed limb 'with other baggage that they called reliques', but they were caught, searched and after being tried at the Guildhall, were executed as traitors. Their revered Prior, Father Houghton, was beatified in 1886 and canonized in 1970.

# HOWARD, KATHERINE, QUEEN

Although diminutive – under five feet in height – Katherine was extremely attractive, with hazel eyes, ruby lips and reddish brown hair; only too conscious of her looks and possessing an amoral attitude to life, she became the fifth wife of Henry VIII at the age of twenty and thereby sealed her fate.

The marriage took place in August 1540, with Katherine seemingly being devoted to her husband; indeed the French Ambassador, writing to the King of France, mentioned how she wore round her arm the motto 'No other will but his'. As has been described in an earlier entry, the couple embarked on a royal progress for the purpose of allowing the people to see the new Queen. The day after their return, Henry was at Mass when Archbishop Thomas Cranmer passed a note to him containing information supplied by the brother of one of Katherine's maidservants, probably for a suitable reward, regarding the many intimate activities involving Mannock and Dereham which had taken place before the royal marriage. Henry's initial reluctance to believe it was quickly replaced by understandable anger, and the Archbishop was tasked with obtaining a full confession from Katherine.

When interrogated, the young woman blurted out everything, admitting how Dereham 'would bring wine, strawberries, apples and other things to make good cheer after the

Duchess of Norfolk [in whose household she was living at the time] had gone to bed.' Then, doubtless terrified and hardly knowing what she was saying, she went on to confess her affair with Thomas Culpepper, not only before, but since her marriage to the King, revealing how, at Lincoln and other places during the royal progress, he had been brought to her bed-chamber (by Lady Rochford) at eleven o'clock at night and had stayed there until four next morning, although she protested that she had not violated any of her marriage vows.

Henry's inevitable reaction was reported in a further letter from the French Ambassador: 'The King hath changed his love for the Queen into hatred and taken such a grief at being deceived, that of late it was thought that he had gone mad, for he called for a sword to slay her, he had loved her so much.' Katherine was immediately confined to her room and Henry never saw her again. There exists a legend that she tried to see her husband to explain, perhaps to plead, attempting one day to enter the Chapel while he was at prayer. She was seized by the guards and carried back, 'while the King, in spite of her piercing screams, which were heard almost over the Palace [Hampton Court] continued his devotions unmoved. The Haunted Gallery takes its name from being supposedly haunted by the shrieking ghost of poor Katherine.'

A few days later, the Queen's guilt was openly announced in the Great Watching Chamber and her household dismissed. She was moved to the Tower of London and charged with treason, in that,

Katherine, Queen of England, late of Lambeth, Surrey, before the marriage between the King and her, had an abominable, base, carnal, voluptuous and vicious life, like a common harlot, with divers persons, maintaining outwardly the appearance of chastity and honesty. That she led the King by word and gesture to love her and – he believing her

to be chaste and pure and free from other matrimonial yoke
– arrogantly coupled herself with him in marriage.

She was attainted (condemned) by both Houses of Parliament,
this receiving the King's assent on 11 February 1542.

Awaiting death in the Tower, nevertheless the twenty-two-
year-old girl resigned herself to her fate and, determined to
retain her dignity and calmness when on the scaffold, incredibly, on the eve of her execution, she called for the block to be
brought to her room and the executioner to be summoned.
With the officers of the Tower watching the macabre
rehearsal, she knelt down and laid her head on the block to
assure herself that she could endure the ordeal with composure on the following day.

At 10 am on 15 February 1542 she was led out on to Tower
Green where six years earlier Anne Boleyn had paid a similar
terrible price. After praying on the scaffold Katherine admitted her guilt and said, 'I die a Queen, but I would rather die
the wife of Culpepper. Good people, I beg you, pray for me.' The
axe fell, only one stroke being needed, and a witness, Otwell
Johnson, wrote to his brother in Calais: 'The Queen made the
moost godly and chrystian end that ever was hard tell of, I
thynke, sins the world's creation.' Her weeping women then
covered her corpse with a black cloth and carried it into St
Peter's Chapel where, placed in a common coffin, it was buried.
She had been married to Henry VIII precisely one year, six
months and four days.

## HOWARD, WILLIAM, VISCOUNT STAFFORD

In September 1678 one Titus Oates, a renegade, Protestant
or Catholic whenever it suited him, reported to a magistrate, and repeated it later before the King and the Privy

Council, that a plot had been concocted to re-establish Catholicism as the main religion, with the help of an invasion by the French. Accused by Oates as conspirators in the 'Popish Plot', as it became known, were many Catholic peers, one being Viscount Stafford. Whatever doubts existed, rapidly dissolved when in the following month Sir Edmundbury Godfrey, the Justice of the Peace to whom Oates had initially reported the affair, was found dead, brutally murdered, in a ditch near Primrose Hill, London. This fanned the already smouldering flames of anti-Papist public opinion and Stafford was committed to the Tower, where he was imprisoned for the next two years until his trial in Westminster Hall in November 1680, Oates being the principal witness against him. Stafford defended himself with dignity, pleading total innocence, but eventually the House of Lords carried the Resolution, 'That this House is content that the Sheriffs should execute William, late Viscount Stafford, by severing his head from his body.'

On a bitterly cold morning four days after Christmas, 29 December 1680, William Stafford was escorted to the public execution site on Tower Hill. Many of the riff-raff lining the route hooted and jeered at the unfortunate man, and when he protested to Cornish, one of the Sheriffs, he received the pitiless reply, 'I am ordered to stop no man's mouth but your own!' However, as he reached the scaffold the spectators there were more sympathetic and shouted words of encouragement to him.

After a prayer he knelt down and placed his head on the block. Jack Ketch, a man who was making his debut as executioner and who would become the epitome of brutality on the scaffold, raised his axe but, instead of striking, lowered it again after a few moments. Stafford had closed his eyes by then, tense and waiting for the impact, but on hearing the shuffling noise as the man moved, opened them again and asked the reason for the delay. 'I am but waiting for your sign,' said the executioner. 'I shall make no sign,' Stafford answered quietly, placing his head on the block again. 'Take your own time.' There was a brief pause, then the executioner struck, one blow sufficing.

Time gave back Stafford his honour but not his life, for within five years Titus Oates was proved to be a perjurer and a liar. The same tribunal of the Lords that had committed Stafford to the block reversed the Bill of Attainder against him and completely vindicated his character. But it couldn't replace his head on his shoulders.

# HUNGERFORD, LORD WALTER

There seems little doubt that this nobleman's family background drastically influenced his personality, its disturbing events overshadowing his adolescent life to the extent that it ultimately brought about his violent demise. Not only did his mother, Jane, daughter of Lord Zouche of Haryngworth and wife of Sir Edward Hungerford, die young (exactly how and when is not known), while Walter was in his teens, but his stepmother Agnes was hanged for murdering her first husband. To understand why he was beheaded, a study of these events is essential.

The leading player in this domestic drama was undoubtedly his stepmother-to-be who, as a villager named Agnes Cottell, was employed by Sir Edward, by then a widower, in some capacity apparently higher up the menial scale than merely a kitchen maid or even housekeeper. The family's country seat was Farleigh Castle (now a ruin, albeit with some splendid remains) situated in a village appropriately named Farleigh-Hungerford near Bath. Sir Edward, Sheriff of Wiltshire, Somerset and Dorset, Commissioner of the Peace and highly regarded in court circles, also owned a magnificent house in London, the family name later being commemorated in the locality by Hungerford Street (in which Charles Dickens, as a child of ten, began his working life by sticking labels on blacking bottles), and Hungerford Stairs. Where the mansion and its gardens once stood, a successor built Hungerford Market, the site now being occupied by Charing Cross Station – from which southbound trains depart across Hungerford Bridge.

To Agnes, a landowner as wealthy and aristocratic as Sir Edward would seem to have been a worthwhile catch; on his part, he might even have intimated to the lady that their relationship could blossom even further were it not for the existence of her husband John. That suspicion was supported by the fact that, on 26 July 1518, at Agnes's bidding, William Inges and William Mathewe, two of Hungerford's servants, murdered the unfortunate John Cottell and proceeded to dispose of all traces of his corpse. And then she married Sir Edward.

The crime went undetected and the new Lady Hungerford became a member of a social life of which she had previously only dreamed. Three years passed and then, on 14 December 1521, Sir Edward made his will. With the exception of a few legacies to various churches and friends, he bequeathed all his goods and property, jewels, plate and valuables to his wife, and also made her the sole executrix. Six weeks later, on 24 January 1522, he died.

Whether Agnes was betrayed by an unsuccessful blackmailer, as was likely, or the authorities' suspicions somehow became certainties, is not known, but on 25 August 1522 the two servants Inges and Mathewe were indicted with:

havng with force and arms made an assault on John Cottell at Farley by the procurement and abetting of Agnes Hungerford, late of Heytesbury in the county of

Wilts, widow, at that time the wife of the aforesaid John Cottell. And a certain linen scarf called a kerchier which the aforesaid William and William then and there held in their hands, put round the neck of the aforesaid John Cottell and with the aforesaid linen scarf did then and there feloniously throttle, suffocate and strangle the aforesaid John Cottell, so that he immediately died, and afterwards the aforesaid William and William did then and there put into a certain fire in the furnace of the kitchen in the Castle of Farley the body of the aforesaid John Cottell, which did then burn and consume it.

Agnes Hungerford was charged with 'well knowing that the aforesaid William Mathewe and William Inges had done the felony and murder aforesaid, did receive, comfort and aid them on 28 December 1518.' It was later recorded that a charge of actually murdering her husband was also brought against her.

The trial took place on 27 November of that year, 1522, Lady Hungerford and her two accomplices being found guilty and sentenced to death. While awaiting execution Agnes, together with her sister as chaperone, was confined in the Tower of London, the records showing that the cost of guarding and providing for them for the duration of their imprisonment was ten shillings a week for the accused and five shillings a week for her companion.

At last, the day of execution arrived, as reported in the *Grey Friars Chronicle*: 'This yere 1523 in Feuerelle the xxth day was the lady Agnes Hungrford lede from the Tower vn-to Holborne and there put in-to a carte at the churchyerde with hare seruantes and so carred vn-to Tyborne, and there all hongyd, and she burryd at the Grayfreeres in the nether end of the myddes of the churche on the northe syde.'

Whether Sir Edward had known or suspected her role in the

shocking affair is open to conjecture; he had, for whatever reason, given her a superior position in the castle while her husband was still alive; Mathewe and Inge were two of his servants and she had access to the castle's furnace. The question arises: how did she account for her husband's disappearance when the subject of marriage between Sir Edward and herself arose – was he an active partner in the plot or just the unresisting victim of a ruthlessly ambitious woman? And if the latter, did he later rebel against her – thereby bringing about his own death?

His son Walter, born in 1503, was similarly favoured by the King. At the age of thirty, he too was appointed Sheriff of Wiltshire, further honours following in 1536 when he was created a peer, taking the title of Lord Hungerford, 1st Baron Hungerford of Heytesbury, and was also given the honorary post of Squire to the Body of Henry VIII. That he was somewhat mentally unbalanced was evidenced by the fact that one of the 'abnormal crimes' he was alleged to have committed was of imprisoning his third wife, Elizabeth, in one of the towers of Farleigh Castle while he committed incest with his daughter. Word of this came to the ears of the authorities, but even more serious a crime, from a political point of view, was that he had communicated with Father Bird, vicar of Bradford, Wiltshire, ordering that cleric to cast a horoscope indicating when the King might die. That reckless act sealed his fate; incest could conceivably be overlooked – high treason, never.

So on Wednesday, 28 July 1540 Lord Walter Hungerford, 1st Baron of Heytesbury, was escorted under heavy guard to the scaffold on Tower Hill where the executioner waited. Some force was evidently necessary to make the condemned man kneel over the block, Stow reporting that 'at the hower of his dethe he seemed so unquiet that many judged him rather frenzie [i.e. out of his mind] than otherwise.'

After the axe had fallen and the vast crowds had dispersed, his body was placed in a coffin and buried in the Royal Chapel of St Peter ad Vincula within the Tower of London. As custom demanded, his head was parboiled, then spiked on London Bridge.

# LAYER, CHRISTOPHER

This gentleman was a Jacobite who, in 1721, went to Rome to unfold a plan to the Pretender which would gain that nobleman the throne; Layer and others would bribe some of the Tower's garrison, then obtain possession of the castle and take the King and the Prince of Wales into custody. Unfortunately for Layer, the plot was discovered and on 18 September 1721 he was arrested. While being taken to a London prison, he managed to escape but again his luck ran out for he was recaptured in Southwark and committed to the Tower. There, extra precautions were taken to ensure that he would not escape again, a Tower officer being ordered to remain in the same building at all times. Nor was that all, for the Secretary of State issued a warrant to the Lieutenant of the Tower stating:

Whereas Christopher Layer, a prisoner in your custody, stands charged upon the oath of several credible witnesses with high treason, and being apprehended for the same did fly from justice and was retaken; and whereas the safe keeping is of the greatest importance to the safety of His Majesty's person and the peace of his realm; these orders are in His Majesty's name to will and require you to cause him, the said Christopher Layer, to be put in irons for the more effectual securing his person in your custody.

On 1 October Layer was brought to the bar of the King's Bench to plead to his indictment for treason and there begged that his heavy leg irons be removed, but the plea was ignored and he was found guilty and sentenced to death. However, the Government thought that the condemned man, being in the shadow of the gallows, might be more willing to furnish further details of the plot, and he was brought back for questioning on subsequent occasions. One such took place on 11 February 1722/3, when he was taken by coach in the company of General Williamson, Deputy Lieutenant of the Tower, and the Gentleman Gaoler, with a marching escort consisting of one officer, one sergeant and twenty-four soldiers, plus ten Yeoman Warders, any prospect of escape thereby being rendered completely out of the question. After more interrogation it was decided that Layer either could not or would not give such information as the Government considered satisfactory and no further reprieve was granted.

On 17 May 1723, nearly seven months after his trial, he was taken to Tyburn, wearing a full dress suit and a tye-wig. On the scaffold he declared his adherence to King James, as he called the Pretender, and advised the people to take up arms on his behalf. After being hanged he was cut down, his head then being severed and displayed on Temple Bar in Fleet Street. There it became the arch's oldest inhabitant, frowning down on the passers-by for more than thirty years, until one stormy night it was blown down into the Strand and picked up by Mr John Pearce, an attorney – somewhat of a coincidence, Christopher Layer in his pre-conspiratorial days having been a barrister of the Middle Temple. Mr Pearce showed his trophy to some friends in a tavern, under the floor of which hostelry it is believed to have been eventually buried.

# LISLE, DAME ALICE

Kind-hearted and charitable, nevertheless Alice Lisle was destined to experience nothing but tragedy in her life, a life brought to a savage end beneath the executioner's axe.

Born about 1614, daughter of Sir White Beckenshaw, in 1630 she married John Lisle, a man who had everything going for him. A barrister, Member of Parliament for Winchester, and so highly thought of by Oliver Cromwell that he was appointed one of those managing the trial of Charles I in 1649. By 1660 he had attained the prestigious post of Commissioner of the Army and Navy, but when Charles II regained the throne, he fled to Switzerland to avoid arrest and possible execution as a regicide, but unknowingly vacated the frying pan for the flames, being later murdered in Lausanne.

After the loss of her husband, Alice continued to live quietly in her house in Moyles Court near Ellingham in Dorset until, in 1685, James, Duke of Monmouth made his rash attempt to gain the throne, leading a would-be army of peasants against James II. The invasion proved abortive and the King, not content with his enemy's defeat, ordered the Lord Chief Justice George Jeffreys, 1st Baron Jeffreys of Wem, to hand out summary justice to the Duke's supporters, a pseudo-judicial process so brutal that afterwards Jeffreys became known as Hanging Judge of the Bloody Assizes. With utter ruthlessness Jeffreys wasted little time in sentencing over 330 people to death. An eyewitness, quoted by Sir Edward Parry, described areas in some southern counties as:

> quite depopulated, nothing to be seen but forsaken walls, unlucky gibbets and ghostly carcases. The trees were loaden almost as thick with human quarters as leaves; the houses and steeples covered as close with heads as at other times with crows or ravens. Nothing could be liker

hell; caldrons hissing, carkases boyling, pitch and tar sparkling and glowing, blood and limbs boyling and tearing and mangling, and Jeffreys the great director of all.

In Lyme Regis, the port at which Monmouth had landed with his meagre force, the mayor was peremptorily ordered to build gallows and provide nooses to hang the prisoners, 'with a sufficient number of faggots to burn the bowels of the traitors and a furnace or caldron to boil their heads and quarters, and salt to boil them with, half a bushell to each traitor, and tar to tar them with, and a sufficient number of spears and poles to fix and place their heads and quarters.'

Hundreds of desperate, panic-stricken men, on the run from the government troops, scattered across Dorset in search of refuge and it so happened that one dark night two men arrived at Dame Alice's door craving shelter. One was a preacher named Hicks, the other a man named Nelthorp. She knew neither of them but despite the appalling risk, she took them in and provided them with food. This humane act signed her death warrant, for a short time later Colonel Penruddock, the local Justice of the Peace, arrived accompanied by a party of soldiers and all three were arrested: Hicks, Nelthorp and their benefactor. The event was reported to Judge Jeffreys who, hell-bent on making an example of his fine catch, went to the extent of obtaining a promise from the King that he would not pardon the lady – even though no trial had yet taken place.

On 27 August 1685 Dame Alice appeared in court on the following charge:

That on 28 July, in the first year of King James II, knowing John Hicks of Keinsham, in the county of Somerset, clerk, to be a false traitor, and to have conspired the death and destruction of the King, and to have levied war against him, did, in her dwelling house at Ellingham, traitorously entertain, conceal and comfort the said John Hicks and cause meat and drink to be delivered to him, against the allegiance, the King's peace, etc. etc.

Alice was extremely deaf, and after the charge had been repeated loudly to her by one Matthew Brown who stood next to her and assisted her where necessary, she pleaded not guilty to the indictment.

For the charge to be sustained it obviously had to be proved first that Hicks was one of Monmouth's men and also that Dame Alice was aware of that, but as far as Judge Jeffreys was concerned all that was a foregone conclusion. The first prosecution witness, Pope, testified that he had been taken prisoner by Monmouth's forces and while captive was visited by Hicks who, although treating him kindly, nevertheless reproached him for being a Protestant but serving a Popish prince, rather than obeying a Protestant King (Monmouth). He also alleged that Hicks had used several other expressions reflecting on the King and Government.

Having proved Hicks had fought for Monmouth, prosecuting counsel Polexfen then proceeded to examine a man named James Dunne. Because he was a reluctant witness he received a fearsome tongue-lashing from Judge Jeffreys who started by threatening him with dire punishment should he vary the truth in any degree. Dunne stated that he lived at Warminster and had been approached by 'a short dark man' who asked him to carry a message from Hicks to Dame Alice, who lived twenty-six miles away, asking her whether she could put Hicks up in her house for a day or two, and for this service, Dunne continued, he would be given a reward. To this he agreed, duly delivering the message, and when asked by the court whether Dame Alice knew Hicks, he said he did not know. However, he continued, a few mornings later two men came to him, identifying themselves as Hicks and Nelthorp and telling him they were being pursued by their debtors. The trio then met a man named Barter who guided them to Dame Alice's house, reaching there that evening.

The need to extract the answers to his questions from the unwilling Dunne was like pulling teeth and had the inevitable effect on the by now apoplectic Judge, who verbally belaboured him, calling him a vile wretch, and exclaiming, 'Thou art a strange, prevaricating, shuffling, snivelling, lying rascal!' and 'Dost thou think, after all the pains I have been at to get answers to my questions that thou can banter me with such sham stuff as this?' And a court official hastily obeyed his Honour when ordered to 'Hold the candle to him that we may see his brazen face!'

Colonel Penruddock testified that Barter had visited him and reported the presence of three suspicious men in Dame Alice's house, whereupon he, together with soldiers, had gone there and on searching the house, found Hicks and Dunne, the latter attempting to conceal himself with some material. Further searches revealed Nelthorp hiding in a hole by the chimney. The colonel stated that he had told Dame Alice that she was committing treason by harbouring the men, to which she replied that she knew nothing about it.

In her defence, Dame Alice stated that she had been willing to shelter Hicks for although she knew warrants were out against him, she did not know he was in Monmouth's army but believed it was because he had been preaching the Protestant faith at private meetings. Furthermore, she declared her utmost loyalty to King James, pointing out that her son was serving with the government forces and making the legal point that she ought not to be tried for harbouring a traitor until that traitor was convicted.

All this had little effect on Judge Jeffreys. Charging the jury as to their verdict, he referred to the damning fact that the prisoner's husband had actually sat in judgement on

Charles I, and that the evidence they had heard 'was as plain as the sun at noonday.' The jury then retired to consider their verdict but returned in half an hour, the foreman saying, 'My Lord, we have some doubt whether she knew Hicks was in the army.' But the Judge, conveniently ignoring the fact that the lady was deaf, replied testily, 'I wonder what it is you doubt of – did not he and Nelthorp discourse of the battle and the army while they were at supper? Come come, gentlemen, it is plain proof!' He sent them out again to reconsider their verdict. Once more they returned, bravely to reiterate their decision – not guilty. Enraged at their apparent disregard of his directions, Jeffreys gave the jury no option and threatened them with dire consequences should they fail to heed his 'judicial recommendation'. At that, the jury, fearing the wrath for which the Judge was renowned, capitulated, and no doubt conscience-stricken but not daring to do otherwise, brought in a verdict of guilty.

On 28 August 1685 Dame Alice was brought to the Bar. Before passing sentence on the old lady, Judge Jeffreys declared that other evidence had come to light, showing her guilty (it is believed that the reason Nelthorp was not charged was because he had given false testimony in order to save his own skin).

Jeffreys advised the prisoner to be penitent and confess, then pronounced sentence that she should suffer death by burning that very afternoon, intimating however that if she would confess, the execution would be delayed (not cancelled!). Although respited until 2 September, she made no confession, but a petition was delivered to King James, His Majesty graciously acquiescing to the plea that the sentence be altered to one of beheading.

Among the crowds that flocked to Winchester's market place to witness such an appalling act inflicted on a frail old lady were many who stated that 'she died with serene courage' as the executioner deftly wielded the axe, only one blow being necessary.

It is of some slight consolation to know that following the Revolution of 1688, when King James fled the country and William and Mary accepted the throne, the judgement passed on Dame Alice Lisle was annulled by Parliament – alas, too late. As for Judge Jeffreys – he was later hunted down and eventually caught. And at thirty-five minutes past four in the morning of 19 April 1689, the cirrhosis of the liver from which he was believed to have been suffering, due to his life-long addiction to brandy, finally proved fatal, and he escaped the axe by dying, unloved and unlamented, in the Bloody Tower.

# LIVINGSTON, JEAN

Wife of John Kincaid, Laird of Warriston, daughter of Livingston of Dunipace, Scotland, Jean Livingston was an attractive woman, twenty-one years of age who, despite, or perhaps because of her beauty, was cruelly treated by her husband, a man much older than her who possessed a fierce and violent temperament. He treated her so badly that eventually she could stand it no longer and made the traumatic decision to have him killed. Accordingly, she persuaded Weir, a manservant of the household, to strangle the laird while he slept. After committing the deed, Weir escaped but was caught and sentenced to be broken on the wheel, a very rare penalty in Scotland. The condemned man was tied spread-eagled on a cartwheel mounted horizontally on a post, each arm and leg then being systematically shattered in two places, above and below the elbow, above and below the knee, by blows dealt by the hangman using a length of timber from a plough, the *coup de grâce* being administered by a final blow to the chest.

Lady Warriston, together with her nurse and a loyal female

servant who were also in the conspiracy, was condemned to die in the usual way for female transgressors, by being secured to a stake surrounded by tinder and matchwood, there to be strangled as the mounting flames caught hold, and their remains burnt to ashes. But following entreaties by Jean's friends, she was granted the concession of being executed by the Scottish Maiden.

To divert those who sympathized with her, not only on account of her youth and beauty, but also because of the harsh treatment she had received from her husband, the execution was planned to take place very early in the morning; as a further diversion her accomplices were to be strangled and burned at exactly the same time. And at 3 am on 5 July 1600 their erstwhile mistress was led to the Girth Cross at the foot of the Canongate in Edinburgh. There, in the fitful light of the flickering torches held by the officials, she knelt submissively – the Lokman stepped forward and pulled the lever – and the severed head of Jean Livingston fell into the waiting basket.


# LUME, SARA

The good citizens of Halifax, Yorkshire, had no qualms about releasing the blade of their Gibbet, whether the person whom it would decapitate on descending was male or female. One such unfortunate woman was Sara Lume, a resident of the town, who suffered that particular method of execution on 8 December 1627. Among other women listed in the town's register were Ux. (Latin uxor meaning 'wife of', women being identified by their husband's name) Thom. Robarts de Halifax on 13 July 1588, Ux. Peter Harison de Bradford decoll. (decollate, to decapitate) 22 February 1602, Ux. Johan Wilson decolata. 5 July 1627 and Ux. Samuel Etall on account of many thefts, beheaded 28 August 1630.

The spectacle of a woman's head being severed apparently made little difference, especially when, as often happened, such was the force of the falling blade that the head was propelled into the crowd. Evidence that this did occur was provided by the Halifax historian Wright who described how a woman, riding along Gibbet Street one day as an execution was taking place, was shocked suddenly to see the head land in the basket she carried in front of her on the saddle. Constant recounting of this event embroidered it further, alleging that the head, missing the basket, gripped her apron and held on with its teeth!

Had these women been able to escape from the town before being caught or even while being led to execution, they would not have been pursued. As Thomas Pennant in his book *Tours*, published in 1776, explained: 'If the criminal could escape out of the limits of the forest, part being close to the town, the bailiff had no further power over him. But if he should be caught within the precincts at any time after, he was immediately executed on his former sentence. This privilege was very freely used during the reign of Elizabeth.'

## McMAHON, HUGH OGE, COLONEL
## MAGUIRE, CORNELIUS, 2nd BARON OF ENNISKILLEN

These two gentlemen were Irish Royalists who, in 1641, were involved in a plot to capture Dublin Castle. The conspiracy failed and after capture they were brought to London and imprisoned in the Tower. There they remained for three years until, one night in August 1644, they managed somehow to obtain possession of a saw with which they cut their way through the wood of their cell door. Hidden by visiting friends near the entrance was a rope which, after mounting to the battlements, they secured to a strongpoint. Then, following instructions which had been smuggled in to them inside a loaf of bread giving details of a light which would signal to them from the far side of the moat, one by one they lowered themselves into the stagnant waters and swam to where their friends were waiting to drag them up the slimy bank and whisk them away to a safe house, the residence of the French Ambassador.

On the following day the hue-and-cry was raised, a reward of £100 being offered by Parliament for their capture. With the threat of a heavy fine hanging over him for negligence of duty, the appropriately named Sir John Clotworthy, Lieutenant of the Tower, made every effort to track down the escapers, eventually locating the house in which they had taken refuge. Although the Ambassador protested vehemently, a committee of both Houses of Parliament authorized a search, and the two prisoners were taken into custody and returned to more secure quarters in the Tower.

At their trial Colonel McMahon was found guilty of high treason and sentenced to be hanged, drawn and quartered, that judicial process being performed at Tyburn. Lord Maguire pleaded that as he was an Irish peer he should be tried in that country but, after lengthy consultation between the judges and lawyers, his plea was overruled and he was condemned to death. His request that as a baron he should be entitled to be beheaded was also rejected by Parliament and on 20 February 1645 he too 'went West' travelling the three miles to Tyburn, there to suffer the same ghastly fate as his erstwhile fellow plotter.

## MARISCUS, SIR WILLIAM OF

The dreaded penalty of being hanged, drawn and quartered was first recorded in 1242, the first known victim being Sir William de Mariscus (or Mariscis or Marsh). An event which led up to it involved an even more barbaric way of being put to death, as reported in Matthew Paris's *Chronicles*:

In 1238 King Henry III, being at Woodstock, a certain learned squire came to the court. He feigned madness and demanded of the King that he should give up the crown. The King's attendants sought to drive him away but the King forbade this. In the middle of the night the man came again, bearing an open knife. He made his way into the King's bedchamber but the King was not there, being with the Queen. But one of the Queen's maids, Margaret Bisseth, was awake and, sitting by the light of a candle, sang psalms, for she was a holy maid, and one devoted to the service of God. Margaret gave the alarm and the man was secured. He declared that he had been sent by William Marsh on purpose to kill the King.

On learning this, the King ordered that, as the one guilty of an attempt to kill the King's majesty, he should be torn by horses, limb from limb, a terrible example, and a lamentable spectacle to all who should dare to plot such crimes. In the first place he was drawn asunder, then beheaded, and his body divided into three parts, each of which was dragged through one of the greatest cities of England, and afterwards hung on the robbers' gibbet.

The would-be assassin's leader, Sir William Marsh, was the son of Geoffrey, Viceroy of Ireland, a doughty warrior who fought against the rebels in that turbulent country and on one occasion had not only taken the King of Connaught prisoner but had left twenty thousand of his followers dead on the field of battle. But when, in 1235, a messenger named Henry Clement was sent by some Irish peers to deliver dispatches to King Henry, only to be murdered on his arrival in London, Geoffrey's son was accused of his death. Nor was that all, for although pleading his innocence, William was also believed by the authorities to be responsible for the attempt on the King's life at Woodstock by one of his underlings, as described above. Sir Geoffrey himself was also suspected of being involved in the attempt and, his estates being confiscated, he fled to Scotland, but the King's agents pursued him and he escaped to the Continent, eventually dying poverty-stricken in France.

The hue and cry being raised, William sought refuge on Lundy, a desolate and impregnable island situated in the Bristol Channel some miles off the Devon coast. There, having collected a gang of fugitives and outlaws, he became a pirate. Secure in his stronghold, for the next six years he waylaid passing merchant ships, plundering them of their precious cargoes of wine and provisions, and by using small fast boats, raided the villages on the mainland, bringing terror and death to the inhabitants.

An all-out frontal assault on the well-defended island was discounted as suicidal, and even were a beachhead established, the stronghold, situated on a high hill and accessible only by climbing a ladder, would have been almost impossible to overwhelm. The King therefore decided that the only strategy was infiltrate the gang, and so offered a large reward. Not all the gang members were voluntary participants and one proved only too willing to double-cross his leader. Accordingly one foggy night in 1241, having left this particular man on watch, Marsh and his companions relaxed in the headquarters, only to be taken completely by surprise by the attacking force and after some resistance, were captured.

They were confined first in Bristol Castle and taken from thence to London, Marsh and four or five of his confederates being imprisoned in the Tower, where the Lieutenant was directed to ensure 'that they should be safely confined in the direst and most secure prison in that fortress, and so loaded with irons, and in such place be kept that there could be no fear of their escape.'

On the eve of St James, 25 July 1242, sixteen members of the gang were put on trial at Westminster, found guilty of piracy and were put to death by being drawn behind horses through the city and hanged at Tyburn.

Sir William himself vainly pleaded not guilty to the charge of attempting to have the King assassinated and that of murdering the messenger, but to no avail; high treason could carry but one penalty. The historian Paris continues the story:

> He was drawn from Westminster to the Tower and thence to that instrument of punishment called a gibbet. When he had there breathed out his wretched soul, he was hanged on one of the hooks and when the body was stiff, it was let down and headed, then disembowelled, and the bowels were burnt on the spot. Then the miserable body was divided into four parts, which were sent to four of the chief cities so that this lamentable spectacle might inspire fear in all beholders.

## MENTEITH, SIR JOHN, EARL OF

As related in a later entry, the Scottish hero and patriot William Wallace was captured in 1305 and brutally executed. He was not taken honourably, in battle, but was betrayed by other defeated Scottish knights who, in exchange for a lesser period of banishment from the kingdom, had agreed to divulge Wallace's whereabouts.

According to tradition one of these was Sir John de Menteith, whose loyalties over the years had alternated between the protagonists on both sides of the border. In 1296 he had been imprisoned for defying Edward I yet eight years later he was Sheriff of the castle, town and sheriffdom of Dumbarton, in which capacity he pleaded in his defence that he had no alternative but to arrest Wallace and hand him over to the authorities in London.

He was later given a seat on the Scottish Council and created Earl of Lennox, but in 1346 he joined David II, King of Scotland who, after spending seven years in the luxury of the French court, had returned to Scotland and, at the behest of Philip of France, invaded England. Sweeping over the border and crushing all opposition, his army headed south, reaching as far as Durham, but defeat at Neville's Cross shattered the royal ambitions, he and his supporters being captured. King David was imprisoned for eleven years and released after an enormous ransom had been paid. His supporters, the Earl of Monteith in particular, were not so lucky, Edward III passing sentence on him from Calais:

*Si est agarde q'ils soient Ajuggez Traitres, &, come Traitres & Tirantz atteintz, Traynez, Penduz, Decolez, & lour Corps Quartirez, & lour Chiefs mys sur le Pount de Loundres, & les Quarters mys a les Quatre Principals Villes du North (c'est assaver) a Everwyk, Noef Chastel sur Tyne, Kardoil, and Berwyk de les y pendre haut par Cheines, en ensample & terrour des Traitres & Tirantz celles Parties.*

Roughly translated, Monteith had been adjudged a traitor and was to be drawn, hanged (Penduz), beheaded (Decolez) and quartered (Quartirez), the quarters to be sent to the principal cities of the north, York (?), Newcastle upon Tyne, Carlisle (?) and Berwick to hang in chains as an example and deterrent to all traitors and tyrants. His head was to be set on London Bridge. And so it was.

# MONTFORT, SIMON of, EARL OF LEICESTER

Simon de Montfort was born in Normandy in about 1208 and at the age of twenty-one came to England where, in 1232, he was confirmed in his inherited title as Earl of Leicester. Six years later he married Eleanor, Henry III's sister, and became heavily involved in politics, his high-handed attitude putting him at odds with the King. And when, in 1261, Henry proclaimed his intention to rule as he pleased, Montfort was chosen by Parliament to lead its forces against the King. Arbitration by St Louis of France having failed, civil war broke out, the Earl and his men defeating the Royalists at the Battle of Lewes in 1264. Prince Edward, the King's son, having been captured and held hostage, Simon seized the opportunity virtually to rule the country and to reform Parliament. This he did by summoning as its members, churchmen, barons and citizens representative of each borough, a system which has developed into its present format.

But his supporters in the country, including his own son, were lawless in the extreme, attacking rich manor houses, stealing timber from their forests and deer from their estates and robbing prominent Royalists. The crisis came to a head with the escape of Prince Edward and the desertion to the Royalists of one of the Earl's closest allies, Gilbert de Clare, Earl of Gloucester. After many skirmishes, the opposing sides finally met in battle at Evesham where, the Prince's close friend the Earl of Mortimer having seized the only bridge, no retreat was possible and in a heavy thunderstorm both forces fought savagely, giving no quarter. The end, when it came, was graphically described by Richard Grafton, the sixteenth-century chronicler and printer:

> The Earl, with great pain [difficulty], passed the bridges before broken by Prince Edward, and so coasted the coun-

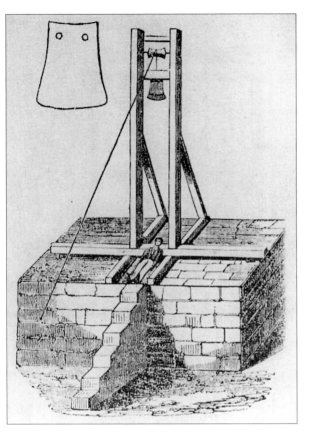

The Halifax Gibbet-Law
*(Above left)*

The Maiden *(Above)*

Heading Block, Axe and Mask
*(Left)*

The Triple Tree, about 1680
*(Above)*

Execution by the sword *(Above)*

Broken on the wheel *(Right)*

Regicides
Hanged,
Drawn and
Quartered;
from a
pamphlet
of 1662

Torture by
the Rack in
the Tower of
London

Hanged,
Drawn and
Quartered

Execution of the Cato
Street Conspirators

Execution of
the Jacobites

Colonel Townley's Head on Temple Bar,
Fleet Street

" Observe the banner which would all enslave,
Which ruined traytors did so proudly wave,
The devil seems the project to despise ;
A fiend confused from off the trophy flies.

While trembling rebels at the fabrick gaze,
And dread their fate with horror and amaze,
Let Briton's sons the emblematick view
And plainly see what to rebellion's due."

COPY OF A PRINT PUBLISHED IN 1746.

Drawbridge Gate of
Old London Bridge

The Martin Tower, Tower of London – the author's ex-residence is in the background *(Above)*

Interior of the Chapel Royal of St Peter and Vincula *(Left)*

Place of Execution, Tower of London *(Below)*

Bloody Tower Archway, Tower of London

Torture by the 'boots'

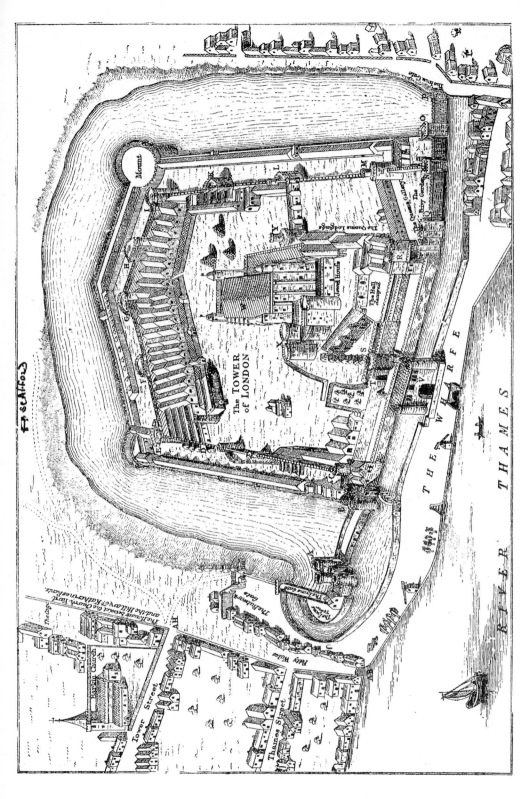

The Tower of London from a survey in 1597

tries in gathering of the people as he went, so that at length he had with him a great power. And when Edward heard thereof, he made towards him as fast as might. And the sixth day of August 1265 they met at Evesham in Worcestershire, where between them was foughten a cruel and bloody battle, in which was slain the said Sir Simon the Earl and many other noble men that held upon his party.

After which discomfiture some malicious person, in despite [contempt] of the Earl, cut off his head and his privy members, and fastened them upon either side of his nose, and after made a present thereof on a pike unto the wife of Sir Roger Mortimer. His feet also and his hands were cut off from the body and sent to sundry places, and the trunk of his body buried within the church of Evesham.

## MORE, SIR THOMAS

Born in 1478, highly intelligent, a brilliant speaker and devoted husband and father, Sir Thomas became Under Secretary, Speaker of the House of Commons, Chancellor of the Duchy of Lancaster and Lord Chancellor. His one great misfortune was that he came to maturity in the reign of Henry VIII, for when the King's divorce from Catherine of Aragon brought about the severence of relations with Rome, More could not accept the monarch's action in becoming the Head of the Church and refused to sign the resultant Act of Succession. Since he was a man of strong and unswerving religious principles, further argument was useless, further attempts at persuasion out of the question. Confinement in the Tower in 1534 did nothing to change his mind, nor did the implicit threat of execution during his trial in Westminster Hall, where he was indicted with 'behaving maliciously and traitorously against the Crown and regall dignity of his sacred Majestie'. Within a quarter of an hour the court, not daring to risk Henry's wrath were they to find otherwise, brought in a verdict of guilty and he was sentenced to death.

Returning to Tower Wharf he was met by his loving daughter, Margaret Roper, who, regardless of the crowds and soldiers escorting him, 'imbraced him and took him about the neck and kissed him, and like one that had forgotten herself, with a full and heavie heart, was fain to depart from him. The beholdinge whereof was to manie that were present soe lamentable that it made them for verie sorrow thereof to weape and mowne.'

On 6 July 1535, early in the morning, the King's message came that he was to die before nine o'clock. When he was told that, because he had held the highest office in the realm, the King had been mercifully pleased to allow him to be beheaded instead of being hanged, drawn and quartered, Sir Thomas laughed and said, 'God forbid the King shall use any more such mercy to any of my friends!'

He put on his best silk camlet (fine wool) gown, but the Lieutenant of the Tower persuaded him to wear something less splendid, for the garments worn by those executed were claimed by the executioner. Accordingly, clad in his old gown made of frieze (a heavy woollen fabric with a long nap used to make coats), his beard long, his face pale, he walked up Tower Hill carrying a red painted cross. On reaching the scaffold he saw that it was in a state of disrepair and, turning to the Lieutenant he said jokingly, 'I pray you, see me safe up, and for my coming down, let me shift for myself!'

After mounting the steps he knelt and repeated the 50th psalm, then kissed the executioner in answer to the man's prayer for forgiveness. 'Pluck up thy spirits, man,' he urged. 'And be not afraid to do thy office. I am sorry my neck is short, therefore strike not awry.' Refusing to have his eyes bandaged, he laid his head on the block and, as recorded by the historian Froude, 'The fatal stroke was about to fall when he signed for a moment's delay while he moved his beard, saying, "Pity that should be cut that has not committed treason," and with such strange words, the strangest perhaps ever uttered at such a time, the lips most famous in Europe for eloquence and wisdom closed for ever.'

One blow of the axe being effective, his body was interred in St Peter's Chapel within the Tower and his head, after being parboiled, was displayed on London Bridge. His great-grand-son describes what happened next in his book on Sir Thomas printed in 1726: 'It was putt where trayters' heads are set vpon poles and hauing remained some tyme there, being to cast into the Thames because room should be made for diuerse others, who, in plentiful sorte, suffered martyrdome for the same supremacie of the King, shortly after it was bought by his daughter Margarett, lest it should be foode for fishes.'

Meg Roper kept it with her until her death ten years later when 'in a leaden box something of the shape of a beehive, open in front', it was placed in a niche in the Roper tomb in St Dunstan's Church, Canterbury. It seems that some time later the lower jaw was stolen, resulting in an iron grille being fixed in the stonework in front of it as a measure of security.

The tomb was entered and inspected in 1715 and again in 1835 during the repaving of the chancel, a visitor then writing how he descended into the vault to ascertain whether the skull was still there. In 1879 the church underwent restoration, and the tomb was visited again. Forty-four years later, in 1930, the then incumbent's wife, Mrs Hoare, entered the tomb and confirmed that the skull was still to be seen behind the grating. The vault was then closed up 'as it was considered undesirable to make it a show place,' that being the last occasion until the most recent inspection of the relic in 1978.

A vertebra from Sir Thomas's neck somehow survived and,

being in the possession of a descendant, Mary, a nun who had taken the name Augusta, was bequeathed by her to the English Convent at Bruges, Belgium. The martyr was beatified in 1886 by Pope Leo and was canonized in 1935, the Church of the Holy Redeemer in south-west London then changing its name to that of the Church of the Holy Redeemer and Saint Thomas More and a segment of the saint's vertebra was kept in a reliquary on the altar. Regrettably this was stolen in 1970 and never recovered.

# NORRIS, HENRY
# WESTON, SIR FRANCIS
# BRERETON, WILLIAM

Flirting with a young lady did not necessarily mean one had to lose one's head over her – but it certainly did if the lady in question was Anne Boleyn and her husband was Henry VIII! The opportunity for this playful, albeit dangerous pastime came about because the King, bitterly disappointed that Anne had given him a daughter instead of the son he so desperately desired as a successor, spent little time with her. However, she had her own small coterie of courtiers to amuse and entertain her, among whom were Henry Norris, Francis Weston and William Brereton. As mentioned earlier (see Boleyn, Queen Anne, p.37) Norris was Groom of the Stole, a Gentleman of the Privy Chamber and a recipient of many favours bestowed on him by the King, who enjoyed the younger man's company. Norris's friend, Sir Francis Weston, a man in his early twenties, had also been honoured, having been created Knight Companion of the Bath at the time of Anne's coronation. William Brereton was another of Anne Boleyn's companions and admirers although, like Norris and Weston, was likely to have been nothing more than that. Also in the company was Mark Smeaton, spinet player and musician, a particular favourite of Anne's, so much a favourite indeed, that according to the malicious rumour-mongers who infested the court, it had been the musician who had called the tune and fathered the Princess Elizabeth, and not the King!

The blow that was to herald the downfall of the Queen and the young men around her, fell on 30 April 1536, when the King's right-hand man, Thomas Cromwell, a political schemer markedly hostile towards Anne, invited Smeaton to his house in Stepney, ostensibly for dinner. Once in the residence, however, the young man lost his appetite when he found himself facing his host across a table with two of Cromwell's henchmen standing behind him. The interrogation began: what did he think of the Queen? What did she think of him? Where did he get the ring he wore? Did she give it to him? Why? What else did he get? How intimately did he know her – had she submitted to him? How often? When? Where? Who else went with her? Were they alone together? Come, answer, answer – we must have answers! And to extract more damning evidence from the petrified courtier, he was taken to the Tower. There, to weaken his resolve, he was first shown the rack, then was secured to the device, the machine that had been terrifyingly described as being capable of stretching the victim a foot taller than God had made him. An exaggerated claim, but one which doubtless felt only too believable to the victim made fast to it. And as the cogs clicked and the ropes strained taut, the confessions flowed from Smeaton, every gasped word, true or false, to be carefully written down and passed to the King.

The following day, May Day, was celebrated by the Tournament at Greenwich, as mentioned earlier, during which Norris picked up a handkerchief Anne had dropped and returned it to her. At the end of the tilting the King abruptly called for Norris to escort him and left the arena. As they rode away, Henry accused Norris of committing adultery with the Queen and was so intent on determining the truth he offered a free pardon, should Norris admit it. The younger man, bewildered and shocked by the charge, denied it vehemently, but to no avail, and on reaching London, he was taken to the Tower, shortly to be joined there by Weston and Brereton.

When interrogated in his prison, Norris repeated his denials of any wrongdoings 'loyally averring that in his conscience he thought the Queen guiltless but, whether she was or not, he was in no position to accuse her of any offence and preferred to undergo a thousand deaths before betrayal of the innocent.' When this rebuttal was reported to the King, Henry is said to have shouted, 'Hang him up, hang him up!'

At their trial in Westminster Hall later in the month, all four, Norris, Weston, Brereton and Smeaton, were charged with being Anne's lovers, though there seems little doubt that the first three men at least, were innocent victims of Cromwell's machinations, and they pleaded not guilty to that charge and also to one of treason. Evidence was given that Mark Smeaton had been seen in the corridor near the Queen's room in Greenwich Palace; faced with this and the confession extracted from him, he pleaded guilty to the charge of adultery. There was little doubt of the outcome, all being found guilty and sentenced to death.

When racked, Mark Smeaton had signed the confession admitting adultery on the promise of being pardoned and released, but the integrity of a Tudor pardon can be judged by the fact that on 17 May 1536 he, being but a commoner, was drawn to Tyburn where, before swinging from the hempen rope, he begged the watching crowd, 'Masters, I pray you all pray for me, for I have deserved the death.' On hearing this virtual confirmation of his guilt, it is reported that Anne exclaimed, 'Did he not clear me of the shame he brought on me? Alas, I fear his soul will suffer for it.'

On the same day his three companions, being Gentlemen of the Court, were granted the privilege of decapitation and so were led out to the scaffold on Tower Hill. There, both Sir Francis Weston and William Brereton spoke with contrition but made no mention of the charges on which they had been found guilty. Henry Norris, resigned to his undeserved fate, said little. And the axe fell on each in turn.

Norris's head was claimed by his relatives and later interred in the private chapel of their manor house of Ockwells near Maidenhead. His body and the remains of the other victims were, according to Wriothesley's *Chronicles*, 'buried within the Tower, Weston and Norys in the churchyeard of the same in one grave, Mr Bruton [Brereton] and Markes [Smeaton] in another grave of the same churchyeard.' The burial ground referred to was the cemetery surrounding St Peter's Chapel and extended to the area where now the Waterloo Block and Jewel House are situated.

## NORTON, CHRISTOPHER
## NORTON, THOMAS

Following a rebellion in the north in 1570, Thomas Norton and his nephew Christopher, both of Yorkshire, were tried and found guilty of high treason for plotting to overthrow the Queen, and on 27 May of that year they paid the awful penalty. A tract entitled *The Confessions of Thomas and Christopher Norton* was published soon afterwards for the benefit of those who unfortunately had not been able to witness the executions for themselves. It read:

On Saturday May 27th, Thomas Norton and Christopher Norton of Yorkshire, both being condemned of high treason, were delivered by the Lieutenant of the Tower to the Sheriffs of London and were both laid on a hurdle and so drawn through the city of London to Tyburn, having besides many officers and a multitude of others, a godly preacher riding besides them. And being come to the place of execution, proclamation was made of the cause of their death.

Thomas Norton, the elder man, was first executed, who took his death in this wise. He being come up and standing upon the cart with rope about his neck, the cart was drawn away and there he hung a certain space and then was taken down, headed and quartered in the presence of his nephew Christopher Norton, who then presently must drink the same cup.

Then the executioner proceeded to carry out the sentence on the younger man. After he had hanged a while, he was cut down, the butcher opened him and as he took out his bowels he [the victim] cried and said, 'Oh, Lord, Lord have mercy upon me!' and so yielded up the ghost.

Then being likewise headed and quartered as the other was, and their bowels burned as the manner is, their heads and quarters were put into a basket provided for the purpose and so carried to Newgate Gaol, where they were parboiled, and afterwards their heads set on London Bridge and their quarters set upon sundry gates of the City of London for an example to all traitors and rebels, for committing high treason against God and their prince. God grant it may be a special warning for all men; and God turn the hearts of all those who are maliciously bent against Elizabeth, our Queen and sovereign of this Realm, and send her a triumphant victory over all her enemies. Amen. God save the Queen.

Without doubt a most effective way to encourage patriotism.

# PARRY, DOCTOR WILLIAM

This Welsh gentleman was a Doctor of Law and a Member of Parliament who, in 1585, conspired with a man named Edmund Neville to assassinate Queen Elizabeth. Neville was heir to the exiled Earl of Westmorland and, on hearing of his ancestor's death he realized that if he double-crossed his partner in crime and turned Queen's Evidence, he might be rewarded by being granted the title and estates that had been forfeited.

When the conspiracy came to the ears of the authorities, Parry was taken to the Tower where, it was stated, he made a voluntary confession. In it he said that five years earlier he had owed a Mr Hugh Hare of the Inner Temple a large sum of money, had broken in the man's house and violently assaulted him. Although tried and condemned, he had managed to get away to the Continent, where he became a Roman Catholic. His association with many Jesuits there had convinced him that the religious problems in England could only be solved by the assassination of the Queen, a deed which, he admitted, he was prepared to undertake, adding that his proposal had been commended by Ragazonio, the Papal Nuncio in France.

On returning to England, he said, he had an audience with the Queen to whom he had revealed the whole plan and even showed her letters he had received from the Cardinal of Como absolving him in the Pope's name from sin, should he succeed in his plan. Her Majesty had not been daunted, he added, but had replied that 'no Catholic should be called in question merely for religion or the Pope's supremacy, provided that they shewed themselves good subjects.' Parry said that he did not intend to offer her any violence if she could be persuaded to deal more favourably with the Catholics, continuing, 'Therefore, lest I should commit the murder, I laid away my dagger as often as I had access to her.' He then admitted that later he had read a book by Cardinal Allen which maintained that it was not only lawful, but in fact honourable to kill excommunicated members of royalty and because he was still not convinced of the Queen's leniency to those of his faith, he and Edmund Neville had conspired to recruit ten horsemen, waylay the Queen when she rode out to take the air, and shoot her.

At his trial at the King's Bench, his confession and the letters from the Papal authorities were read out, and he pleaded guilty to the charge of high treason. But when he was sentenced to be hanged, drawn and quartered, he delivered a fierce tirade against the Queen, saying that her blood would be answerable for his death. At this the court was in uproar, 'the people shouting, "Away with the Traitor, away with him!" '

On 2 March 1584/5, he was handed over to the sheriffs of London and Middlesex and drawn on a hurdle to Old Palace Yard at Westminster, where he was made to stand in a cart beneath the gallows, a noose about his neck. As Parliament was assembled at the time, many of the peers and members of the Commons came out to witness the execution, and being given leave to address them,

> He impudently denied that he was ever guilty of any intention of killing the Queen, saying that, 'If my hand, my foot, my leg, my arm and all parts of my body would accuse me, my heart is clear and my conscience would acquit me, and if I might be restored my life, then had I all the possessions of the Duchy of Lancaster I would not enjoy them if it meant the loss of a drop of blood from her little finger.' But his plea availed him naught and without any request to the people to pray for him, or using any outward prayer himself, he was turned off, drawn, headed and quartered, according to sentence.

Should it be wondered whether one could remain conscious

while being disembowelled, the ghastly fate of William Parry might well provide some evidence, for it was recorded that 'as the cart was drawn away from under him, the executioner caught the rope at the first swing and butchered him alive, and when his heart was taken out, he gave a great groan.

# PECKHAM, HENRY

At best, Henry Peckham was intensely patriotic; at worst he was unable to resist the lure of £50,000 which, in 1555, or indeed in any century, was a lot of money. Whatever his motive, his eventual appointment with the executioner was unavoidable, his fate a foregone conclusion.

Coming from a good family – his father, Sir Edmund Peckham was Master of the Tower Mint – Henry became Member of Parliament for Chipping Wycombe in 1552–3 and 1555. The topic of conversation in the family household in all probability being mainly of a financial nature, doubtless he pricked up his ears on hearing that Philip of Spain was bringing the aforementioned large sum of money as a gift for his new wife, Queen Mary.

It so happened that at that time, Peckham was involved in a conspiracy to mount an insurrection against the Queen and, as is well known, recruits willing to march, shout inflammatory slogans and attack troops and palaces, are particularly loth to do so without first receiving cash in hand. In order to raise the necessary funds he, together with colleagues John Daniell, John Dethick, Richard Uvedale, John Throckmorton and William Stanton, planned to raid the Exchequer's treasury and steal the money, but all were apprehended when another of the plotters, White by name, turned informer. Other conspirators fled to France (see Stafford, Thomas) but Peckham and his companions were found guilty of high treason and duly paid the price.

Throckmorton and Uvedale suffered at Tyburn on 28 April 1556, Stanton dying likewise on 19 May. Dethick was executed on 8 June, and on Tuesday 7 July, Daniell and Peckham were hanged and beheaded on Tower Hill. Henry Peckham's head was set on London Bridge and his body interred in the nearby church of All Hallows by the Tower.

## PLUNKET, OLIVER, ARCHBISHOP OF ARMAGH

In 1678 the political situation was tense. The sound of Dutch guns had been heard in the Thames and the French were suspected of massing a great army preparatory to invading England in order to impose popery and poverty. King Charles had no successor in direct line and when he died, the crown would pass to his brother James, known to be a Catholic. It was a time when wild and unfounded rumours were circulated and believed, when the Popish Plot invented by the fanatic Titus Oates was accepted by many without question. The word went round that the Plot had to be handled as if it were true, whether it was or not; that those who were allegedly conspiring against the King and aiding the French, had to be summarily tried, found guilty and executed.

Among those who were convicted on perjured evidence was Oliver Plunket, Archbishop of Armagh (see also Howard, William, Viscount Stafford, p.127). Accused of planning to organize the landing of French troops in Ireland, the Archbishop was found guilty of high treason and sentenced to be hanged, drawn and quartered. On 1 July 1681 he was dragged to Tyburn and there hanged by Jack Ketch but cut down while still alive and then disembowelled, his heart and other organs being thrown on to the fire prepared in readiness.

When the ghastly procedure at the scaffold was complete, what mutilated parts of the body which could be salvaged were placed in a coffin and in compliance with orders issued by Charles II, carried to the cemetery of St Giles in the Fields, a church situated near the junction of Oxford Street and Tottenham Court Road. The funeral service was read by Abbot Maurus Corker who had been a fellow prisoner of the Archbishop while both were imprisoned in Newgate Gaol. A copper plate buried with the coffin was inscribed: 'In this tomb resteth the body of the Right Rev. Oliver Plunket, Archbishop of Armagh and Primate of Ireland, who in hatred of religion was accused of high treason by false witnesses, and for the same condemned and executed at Tyburn the first of July 1681, in the reign of Charles II.'

Two years later the remains were exhumed and taken by the Abbot to the Benedictine Abbey of St Adrian at Lamspringe, near Hildesheim in Germany where they stayed until 1803 when, other than for one large relic, they were interred in the graveyard there. In 1883 the remains were again moved, this time to St Gregory's Monastery at Downside, Bath.

Yet another relic, one of the two arms amputated below the elbows by Father Corker prior to the original burial in 1681, was first preserved at Samsfield Court, Herefordshire, but was later taken to a Franciscan convent at Taunton in Somerset. The whereabouts of the other arm is not known.

Miraculously, however, an even holier relic had survived. While all eyes were on the appalling mutilation taking place at the scaffold, the Archbishop's severed head was surreptitiously removed from the basket and hastily smuggled away through the crowd, eventually being sent by devious means to Cardinal Howard in Rome, who later presented it to Archbishop Hugh McMahon. In 1722 that worthy cleric brought it to Ireland, together with the coffin-plate, a visitor to the Siena Convent in Drogheda in the 1920s describing how, within a silver and ebony casket, the head lay on a cloth, the eyes closed, the features relaxed in peace and dignity. The dark brown skin was perfectly preserved, although part of the left cheek and a little of the upper lip were burnt black, scorched by the Tyburn fire which had also singed most of the sparse hair still covering the skull. Across the top of the head the mark of a deep cut was apparent, perhaps the result of a badly aimed blow by Ketch when severing the head. To end on a less savage note, it was reported that a sweet and unidentifiable perfume was sometimes emitted, scenting the air for some minutes after the shrine had been opened.

## POLE, WILLIAM de la, DUKE OF SUFFOLK

Even having the King of England on your side is no guarantee that you'll save your neck, as William de la Pole found to his cost in 1450. Although one of the most able soldiers of his time, having served valiantly under Henry V and being created Duke of Suffolk by his son Henry VI, William, probably through no fault of his own, had been forced to surrender to Joan of Arc at Orleans twenty years earlier. Because of subsequent defeats by the French, for which he was blamed, he proved an easy target, not only for his many enemies at court, led by the Duke of York, but also by the public at large.

As the opposing faction grew stronger and more determined to remove one so favoured by the King, various charges were levelled against him, one ludicrous accusation being that he had planned to send ammunition and military equipment to the French. On 9 March 1450 he was brought before the Bar of the House of Lords to answer the charges but, instead of allowing the hearing to continue in the proper way, which would probably have resulted in his being tried and found guilty of treason, the King exercised his prerogative and without consulting the peers, sentenced Pole to be banished from the country for five years.

Wasting little time, the Duke travelled by coach to the coast and there embarked for Calais in one of a small flotilla which consisted of two ships and a pinnace, some of his most trusted men being sent on ahead in the latter craft bearing letters to the French authorities to ascertain whether their master would be received cordially and given the necessary sanctuary. But his sworn antagonist the Duke of York was not going to let his enemy escape so easily and on his orders, the *Nicholas of the Tower*, one of the largest ships of the English Navy, intercepted the pinnace and after establishing the whereabouts of the parent ships, proceeded to make contact with them. Approaching his prey, the master of the *Nicholas* sent his boat across to that of the Duke of Suffolk and challenged those on board to identify themselves. The Duke himself replied that he was travelling by the King's command to Calais but the master demanded the presence of the Duke as proof, so the nobleman, together with two or three of his men, rowed across to the warship, only to be greeted by the master saying triumphantly, 'Welcome, traitor!'

According to some authorities, a kangaroo court was then held, before which he was arraigned, tried and speedily found guilty. What happened next is best conjured up in correspondence from one William Lowner to the renowned letter-writer John Paston:

The Duke asked for the name of the ship on which he stood, and when told it was *Nicholas of the Tower*, he remembered Stacey, a fortune teller, had said that if he might escape 'the danger of the Tower' he should be safe. Then his heart failed him and, in the sight of all his men he was drawn out of the great ship into a boat; and there was an axe and a stock. One of the lewdest [meanest] of the ship bade him lay down his head and exclaimed, 'He should be fairly dealt with, and die on a sword.' And took a rusty sword and smote off his head within half a dozen strokes, and took away his gown of russet and his doublet of velvet mailed, and laid his body on the sands of Dover. Some say his head was set, appropriately on a pole.

# RADCLYFFE, CHARLES

During the Jacobite Uprising of 1715 Charles and his elder brother James, Earl of Derwentwater (see following entry) fought valiantly against the English, but early in November, having penetrated as far south as Preston, the Scots had to take up a poorly defended position in a churchyard. Charles in particular resisted to the end, exclaiming that 'he would have rather died sword in hand like a man of honour, than yield to be dragged like a felon to the gallows, there to be hanged like a dog.' But overwhelmed by superior forces, both brothers were taken prisoner and, together with the Earl of Nithsdale and other Scottish lords, were escorted to London under heavy guard, their hands tied behind their backs. Charles was confined in Newgate Gaol but on 11 December 1716 he disguised himself by wearing a false brown wig and escaped. He managed to reach France where he joined other fugitive Jacobites and, as the years passed, became the confidant and trusted secretary of the exiled Prince Charles Edward Stuart.

In 1745, he and his son James Clement, together with other Scots, Irish and French officers, while en route to Montrose on board a French ship, the *Espérance* (previously called the *Soleil*) laden with weapons and ammunition for the latest uprising, were captured off the Dogger Bank by the English frigate *Sheerness*. Escorted into Deal, Charles was taken to London to await trial, 'it being sufficient to prove that he is the individual person condemned for the last rebellion, and thence to Tyburn.'

A contemporary described him as 'a man of Boistrous temper with much pride and overbearing conduct', and this was borne out by reports from the Tower that 'his character was so offensive that the Yeoman Warders could be scarcely induced to give him their attendance.' To save money (prisoners had to pay for their keep) he reduced his expenses from seven to five guineas a week by going without suppers, and petitioned that he 'be Remov'd to a worse Prison not so Honourable nor Expensive'.

In court he behaved with great haughtiness and arrogance, proclaiming himself to be Le Comte de Derwentwater (he was the titular Earl of Derwentwater following the execution of his elder brother and the confiscation of the family estates) and claimed to be a French subject and not the young man sentenced to death thirty years earlier. But prosecuting council produced three witnesses who identified him by a scar he bore on his cheek, and Charles's fate was finally sealed when a barber, described in court as 'the close shaver of Newgate Gaol', recognized him as a prisoner he had shorn in that prison in 1716. Found guilty, he was sentenced to be beheaded and so, wearing a scarlet suit faced with black velvet over a gold-laced waistcoat, crimson breeches, white silk stockings and flaunting a white feather in his hat, at the age of fifty-one he was beheaded on Tower Hill by executioner John Thrift. Despite being given ten guineas as an incentive to aim accurately, Thrift, a temperamental and highly emotional hangman – at an earlier execution he had fainted on the scaffold and had to be revived with a glass of wine – needed to deliver three blows with the axe before decapitation was complete.

After the execution, Charles's corpse was carried by friends first to the Nag's Head tavern in Gray's Inn Lane and then, after drinks for the thirsty pall-bearers, taken to be buried at St Giles in the Fields where, despite being surrounded by a rabble demonstrating against a 'papist' being buried there, the interment finally took place, the coffin bearing the invocation 'Requiescat in Pace'.

## RADCLYFFE, SIR JAMES, EARL OF DERWENTWATER

A s described in the previous entry, James and his younger brother Charles were captured with other Jacobite leaders at Preston in 1715, the two reportedly fighting their English opponents like Trojans. Sir James even stripped off his coat and waistcoat so as to move more freely, and promised the sappers more money if they would dig the entrenchments deeper and faster. After their defeat, James, being an earl, was imprisoned in the Tower rather than in Newgate, and when, on 19 February 1716, he was tried in Westminster Hall, he confessed his guilt, pleading that 'he rashly and without premeditation engaged in the affair'. He was sentenced to death, Lord Cowper, the Lord High Steward saying:

And now nothing remains but that I pronounce upon you, and sorry I am that it falls to my lot to do it, that terrible sentence of the law, which must be the same that is usually given against the meanest offenders in the like kind. The most ignominious and painful parts of it are usually remitted by the grace of the Crown to persons of your quality, but the law in this case being deaf to all distinctions of persons, requires that I pronounce the sentence . . .

which, for high treason, was that of being hanged, drawn and
quartered.

However, the Crown *did* remit the penalty to one of being
beheaded and, on 24 February 1716, the twenty-eight-year-old
Earl met his end on a high, specially built and black-draped
scaffold on Tower Hill. Equally funereal was his velvet suit, his
hose and high-heeled leather shoes, the latter adorned with
silver buckles. Over the flaxen curls of his long wig he wore a
wide-brimmed beaver hat with a black plume, but despite the
finery he was seen, hardly surprisingly, to be very pale as he
ascended the steps. After praying, he declared in a firm and
steady voice that he died a Roman Catholic and regretted
having pleaded guilty and expressing contrition at his trial, for
he acknowledged none but King James III as his rightful
sovereign.

He inspected the block and, noticing a large splinter that
might hurt his neck, told the executioner, a brawny ex-black-
smith named William Marvell, to chip it off with the axe.
Removing his coat and waistcoat, he told the executioner he
would find his fee in the pockets 'to pay him for his trouble',
then positioned his head on the block, advising Marvell to
strike after hearing him say, 'Lord Jesus, receive my soul.' The
executioner obeyed, expertly decapitating his victim with one
stroke.

Some of the Earl's servants then mounted the platform and,
wrapping the head in a large kerchief, they swathed the body
in a black cloth and carried the remains back into the Tower.
Meanwhile, Jacobite sympathizers in the crowd pressed
forward to soak their napkins and handkerchiefs in the blood
which dripped between the boards, blood to be treasured as
relics of the martyr who had died for the Stuart cause.

Contrary to the usual practice, James's head, instead of
being displayed on London Bridge, was placed in a coffin with
his body and first taken to a private Catholic chapel at

Dagenham Park near Romford, where his ghost is still reputed to walk in the grounds. The remains were later moved to Dilston Castle near Hexham in Northumberland and there placed in the family vault.

On the night of his execution the Aurora Borealis was unusually brilliant, Scottish folk attributing it to heaven's wrath and ever after referring to the display as 'Lord Derwentwater's Lights'. It was also reported that the local peasantry blamed his wife, the Countess, for making her husband join the Jacobites, she having told her lord that 'it was not fitting that an Earl of Derwentwater should continue to hide his head in hovels from the light of day when the gentry were up in arms for the cause of their rightful sovereign.' She then made her point even more forcibly by throwing her fan at him and exclaiming, 'Take that, and give me your sword!' Rising against her, the locals drove her from her home on Lord's Island; the valley through which she is supposed to have fled was afterwards known as 'Lady's Rake'.

In 1805 the family vault was opened, the coffin lid removed and the public allowed to view the remains. One visitor, quoted by the author Richard Davey in his book *The Tower of London* published in 1910, described what he saw: 'The hair was quite perfect, the features regular and wearing the appearance of youth. The marks of the axe were visible and the shroud but little decayed.' Reverence for the dead, however, gave way to commercialism when a local blacksmith stole some of the Earl's teeth and sold them for two shillings and sixpence each! As a result of such sacrilegious vandalism, the vault was sealed and secured.

Twenty or so years later, during the repair of a wall, the vault was reopened and, concealed beneath the coffin, a casket was found which contained the Earl's heart and other internal organs. This was placed in a more appropriate position and the mausoleum once more closed. A further discovery was made in

1842 at Thorndon in Essex, Lord Petrie's residence, when an oak chest which had been made on the Countess's orders and bearing an inscription in brass, was opened and found to contain the clothes worn by her husband on the scaffold, minus those claimed by the executioner, of course. Unusually, Derwentwater's execution was one of the few in which the block was covered with a cloth, and this was discovered with the garments, the blood-stiffened material torn where the axe blade had struck after severing the victim's head.

## RALEIGH, SIR WALTER

Courtier, buccaneer, explorer, adventurer, Captain of the Royal Bodyguard, Sir Walter's future and fortune could have been assured had not Queen Elizabeth I died, for despite the disparity in their ages and personalities, he was very much her favourite. But on the accession of James I, Raleigh was virtually a doomed man. James, already prejudiced against Raleigh, jealous of the man's elegant bearing and his overwhelming confidence within court circles, was even further antagonistic in view of Raleigh's hostility, openly expressed during Elizabeth's reign, to the suggestions that James should succeed her. Nor was the King the only one planning Raleigh's downfall; other members of the court, the Cecils in particular, being determined to remove him from power. And in a matter of weeks following James's accession, Raleigh and others were not only charged with conspiring to place Lady Arabella Stuart, the King's cousin, on the throne but also with betraying England's interests to Spain.

In November 1603 Raleigh was sentenced to death but, fearing the public's violent reaction should one of their heroes be executed, James reprieved Sir Walter and instead sent him to the Tower of London. And there he stayed – for thirteen years.

Initially, he was allowed the company of his wife (his son, Carew, was born in the Tower) and three servants. He was charged £5 weekly for 'food, coal and candle' and confined in the Bloody Tower, although given the freedom to walk along the adjoining battlement, now named 'Raleigh's Walk', from where he would wave and call to his friends walking on the Wharf. But in 1605 the Lieutenant, William Waad, clamped down and he lost these privileges, so he devoted his time to writing and experimenting with chemistry.

As the years went by he despaired of ever obtaining his release, until he finally hit on the idea of bribing James by promising that if allowed to lead an expedition to Guiana he would bring back much treasure, the greater part of which would go to the King. James, aware that Guiana was already claimed by Spain, realized that this was his chance to rid himself of this thorn in his side and promptly set the trap by passing on to Gondomar, that country's Ambassador, every detail of Raleigh's expedition and where the great silver mine in 'El Dorado' on the banks of the Orinoco was supposed to be, promising that if any Spanish subjects were harmed or property encroached upon, Raleigh would be handed over to Spain to deal with as they thought fit.

At the end of March 1617 Raleigh sailed away in a fleet of fourteen ships, taking with him nine hundred men but, on arrival many months later, was so ill that he stayed on board and sent Laurence Kemys, his commander, up the Orinoco with a large body of men. Disastrously, the party encountered a Spanish camp manned by armed men who had been warned in advance of the English expedition. A fierce fight ensued in which Raleigh's son Walter was killed. The Spaniards were defeated and the camp taken – but there was no silver, no treasure, only swamps and jungle, fever and disease. On their return to the small fleet, now down to five ships in number, Raleigh was in despair at the loss of his son and the failure of his mission. Kemys retired to his cabin and committed suicide; Raleigh, knowing the fate that awaited him in England, nevertheless sailed home in a ship ominously named *Destiny*.

On his return in August 1618 he was immediately imprisoned in the Tower once more. James was by now well advanced in a plan to marry Prince Charles, the heir to the throne, to the Spanish Infanta and thereby unite the two countries, so decided that Raleigh must be eliminated at all costs. After much deliberation with his closest advisers he issued a warrant for the reaffirmation of the death sentence that had been passed at Winchester in 1603.

Sir Walter Raleigh was executed in Old Palace Yard in Westminster at eight o'clock in the morning on 29 October 1618, Lord Mayor's Day 'so that the pageants and fine shewes might draw away the people from beholding the tragedie of one of the gallantest worthies that ever England bred.' Early that morning his warder had brought him a cup of sack and asked whether he enjoyed it, to which Raleigh replied that it was a good drink, if a man could tarry over it. And later when a friend of his complained that he couldn't get near the scaffold, Raleigh riposted, 'I know not what shift you will make – but I am sure to have a place!'

On the scaffold he gave a long speech, protesting against the allegations made against him and denying any disloyalty to his King or country. Then gently touching the axe, he said sombrely, 'This is a sharp medicine but it will cure all ills,' and after taking off his gown and doublet, he knelt over the block. There was some little dispute about having him face the east, but he answered, 'If the heart be straight, it is no matter which way the head lieth.' He then urged the executioner, 'What dost thou fear? Strike, man, strike!' And the man had, indeed, to strike twice.

After his decapitation, writes the historian Arthur Cayley: 'the head, after being shown on either side of the scaffold, was put into a red leather bag, over which Raleigh's wrought velvet gown was thrown, and the whole conveyed away in a mourning coach by Lady Raleigh.' It was placed in a case and preserved by her during the next twenty-nine years and when she died, her son Carew kept it in his possession until eventually it was reportedly buried with him at West Horsley, Surrey. Raleigh's body was buried in the chancel near the altar of St Margaret's, Westminster.

# RIGBY, JOHN

Seven miles or so south-west of Chorley in Lancashire in pleasant undulating country lies the village of Mawdesley, and at the foot of Harrock Hill there once stood the ancient Hall in which John Rigby was born in 1570. When, during the reign of Elizabeth I, the campaign against Roman Catholics was in full force, Rigby was one of the staff of a Catholic family, the Fortescues, and appeared on behalf of one of the daughters who had been summoned to appear at Newgate but was too sick to appear personally. She had been summoned 'for causes of religion' and when questioned by the Bench as to his religion, Rigby admitted to being a Catholic himself, though neither a priest nor a papist. But when asked whether he had been reconciled to the Church of Rome, unaware of the law then in force that made such reconciliation high treason, he agreed that he had been. Within minutes he had been put in irons with fetters about his legs, and he was taken to a gaol situated near London Bridge on the south side of the River Thames to await execution; it was the Clink, a gaol so infamous that its very name became a slang name for prison, and which survives today as a penal museum.

In the Clink he met John Gerard, one of the leading Jesuits in England, a man who, until his capture, had been hunted far and wide. And with Gerard's spiritual support and encouragement, John Rigby prepared to meet his Maker as a devout and dedicated Roman Catholic. Gerard was later transferred to the Tower from which, miraculously, he managed to get away (see my *Great Escapes from the Tower of London*, published by Hendon) but John Rigby was not so fortunate, being condemned to be hanged, drawn and quartered at St Thomas Waterings, in those days a marsh about two miles outside London.

As he was being dragged along Borough High Street and the Great Dover Road on 21 June 1600, he replied to one who questioned him about his crime, 'I am a poor gentleman of the House of Harrock in Lancashire; my age is about thirty years and my judgement and condemnation to this death is only and merely for that I answered the judge that I was reconciled, and for that I refused to attend the Protestant Church.' He then disclosed the divine secret, that he had preserved his virginal purity to the end, causing his questioner to say admiringly, 'I see that thou hast worthily deserved a virgin's crown and I pray God send thee the kingdom of heaven, and desire thee to pray for me.'

At the scaffold, which stood where now the Old Kent Road joins Peckham Park Road, his fine physique was the cause of intense suffering for, as described in Challoner's *Memoirs of Missionary Priests*:

After he had been cut down, he stood upright on his feet like a man a little amazed, till the butchers threw him down. Then, coming perfectly to himself he said aloud and distinctly, 'God forgive you. Jesus, receive my soul.' And immediately another cruel fellow standing by, who was no official but a common porter, set his foot upon Mr Rigby's throat and so held him that he could speak no more. Others held his arms and legs while the executioner

173

dismembered and embowelled him, and when he felt them pulling out his heart, he was yet so strong that he thrust the men from him who held his arms. At last they cut off his head and quartered him . . . The people going away complained very much of the barbarity of the execution, and generally all sorts bewailed his death.

## RUSSELL, LORD WILLIAM

As in the case of Archbishop Oliver Plunket, Lord William Russell, commonly known as the 'Patriot', was the victim of perjury, being accused in 1683 of participating in the Rye House Plot, a conspiracy to assassinate Charles II and James, Duke of York near the Rye House Farm in Hertfordshire, as the royal brothers returned from Newmarket races, in order to ensure that the next monarch would be a Protestant.

That the tide of judicial opinion was flowing strongly against him became evident at his trial at the Old Bailey on 13 July 1680, Council for the Crown being the infamous George Jeffreys, who later became the Hanging Judge of the Bloody Assizes, for when Lord Russell asked for a postponement as some witnesses had not arrived, he received short shrift. 'Postponement!' exclaimed the Attorney-General. 'You would not have given the King an hour's notice for saving his life! The trial must proceed.' It did, but purely as a formality, the sentence of being hanged, drawn and quartered being passed although later reduced to one of decapitation.

Strenuous measures were taken to save his life but mercy was out of the question. Lord Russell's father, the Duke of Bedford, offered, through the Duchess of Portsmouth, the King's mistress, the astronomical sum of £100,000 for his son's release, but to no avail. 'If I do not kill him, he will soon kill me!' the King is reputed to have said. Lady Russell, loyal to the very end, went to court and threw herself at the King's feet, imploring him by the memory of her father, the Earl of Southampton, who had been a staunch friend to Charles I, to use the royal prerogative on her husband's behalf. But the King was implacable; Lord Russell must die.

On the day of execution, 21 July 1680, the condemned man was attended by his spiritual adviser, Bishop Burnet, who later wrote:

> Lord William prayed by himself in his chamber, then came out to me; he drunk a little tea and some sherry. He wound up his watch and said, now he had done with time, and was going to eternity. He asked what he should give the executioner; I told him ten guineas; he said with a smile, it was a pretty thing to give a fee to have his head cut off. When the Sheriffs called him at about ten o'clock, I went in the coach with him to the place of execution in Lincoln's Inn Fields. Some of the crowd filling the street wept, while others insulted; he was touched with the tenderness that the one gave him, but did not seem at all provoked by the other. He was singing psalms a great part of the way, and said he hoped to sing better very soon. As he observed the great crowds of people all the way, he said, 'I hope I shall soon see a much better assembly.'

On the scaffold he denied the charges laid against him and begged forgiveness. After repeating a few words of Psalm 147 he removed his peruke (wig), cravat and his coat and, giving the executioner ten guineas, told the man not to wait for a sign. He knelt, positioned his head and the axe descended – not once but twice. Even then, because the weapon had embedded itself in the block, the executioner had perforce to complete the decapitation by severing the few remaining sinews with his knife.

# SCOTT, JAMES, DUKE OF MONMOUTH

James Scott, a young man of charm, good looks and popularity, was born in 1649, the illegitimate son of Charles II and Lucy Walters, and so conceivably considered himself the rightful heir to the throne. When his father died on 6 February 1685, the Duke left Holland, where he had been living with his paramour, Lady Henrietta Wentworth, and on 11 June landed in Lyme Regis, Dorset. There he issued a declaration calling his uncle James II a traitor and usurper and offered to call a free Parliament. When word of this challenge reached London, the authorities promised a reward of £5000 to anyone who would kill him.

Although disembarking with but 150 men he managed to raise a force of local dissidents and supporters to march on London, where he expected to be welcomed with open arms and an invitation to occupy the throne as a Protestant monarch in place of the Catholic James. And had it not been for the accidental discharge of a pistol, members of the present royal family could well have descended from one whom his supporters had proclaimed as 'King Monmouth', the title being chosen to distinguish him from his uncle, King James.

But his ambitions were thwarted and his fate ultimately decided when, his forces preparing to make a night attack on the royal army at Sedgemoor on 6 July 1685, reportedly one of his men inadvertently fired his pistol. The shot alerted an 'enemy' outpost, the alarm was sounded, and battle was joined. Under withering fire from the carbines of the King's army, Monmouth's mounted troops faltered and scattered leaving the infantrymen, the foot-soldiers, of both sides to engage in hand-to-hand fighting. But being inadequately armed, poorly led and eventually outflanked, Monmouth's men were doomed and the Duke, rather than accept defeat, galloped away, abandoning his followers to their fate, two thousand being killed on

176

the battlefield. The diarist John Evelyn described most of those slain as being Mendip-miners who did great execution with their tools and sold their lives dearly, but they were perhaps the more fortunate ones compared to the three hundred or so erstwhile supporters and sympathizers who were later rounded up and sentenced by the 'Hanging Judge' Jeffreys in the Bloody Assizes, to be brutally executed, many being hanged, drawn and quartered (see Lisle, Dame Alice, p.135).

Monmouth fled as far as the New Forest, where he was later captured hiding in a ditch, concealed with ferns, and so the reward was distributed betwen the victorious militia. The captive had disguised himself as a peasant, having exchanged his elegant clothes with a cottager in the woods; without weapons, muddy, exhausted and hungry – raw peas were found in his pocket – his only other belongings consisted of his purse and watch, together with his insignia of St George. Somehow he had retained two small manuscript books, one a treatise on fortification, the other a collection of recipes and charms, the latter containing spells to avoid being wounded in battle – which apparently worked, and others to open cell doors – which, when the Duke was later incarcerated in the Tower of London, failed miserably!

On arriving in the capital he begged King James for an interview. Once in James's presence, Monmouth threw himself on his knees before the monarch and with tears in his eyes pleaded for mercy, concluding pathetically, 'Remember, Sir, I am your brother's son and if you take my life, it is your own blood that you will shed.' But it was stated that 'the King turned from him and bid him prepare for death.' Indeed, so disgusted was James at the Duke's craven attitude that in a letter to the Prince of Orange he wrote: 'The Duke of Monmouth seemed more concerned and desirous to live, and did behave himself not so well as I had expected, nor do as one ought to have expected from one who had taken upon him to be King. I have signed the warrant for his execution tomorrow.'

To obviate the need for a long-drawn-out and unnecessary trial, a Bill of Attainder was raised, charging him with 'high treason in levying war against the King and assuming a title to the Crown'. He was found guilty and sentenced to death.

On 15 July 1685 he was taken up to Tower Hill, not only with the usual escort but also accompanied by three officers, each carrying a loaded pistol, with orders to shoot him dead should an escape bid be attempted. It was reported that the concourse of spectators was incalculable, and his popularity was such that his appearance was greeted with sighs, tears and groans.

On the black-draped scaffold he gave the Sheriffs a document, the contents of which, many said, were never disclosed; instead, a paper issued later by the authorities and purporting to be the one handed over by the Duke, read: 'I declare that the title of King was forced upon me and that it was very much contrary to my opinion when I was proclaimed. For the satisfaction of the world I do declare that the late King told me that he was never married to my mother. Having declared this, I hope that the King who is now, will not let my children suffer on this account.' The authenticity of this document is suspect, not least in view of his vehement claims to the throne at Taunton.

Turning away from the officials, he then gave Jack Ketch, the executioner, six guineas, saying, 'Pray do your business well; do not serve me as you did my Lord Russell. I have heard you struck him three or four times – if you strike me twice I cannot promise not to move.' He also told his servant to give the executioner six more guineas if the man did his work well.

Having taken off his coat and wig, and refusing to have his face covered, he fitted his neck to the block but soon raised himself on his elbow and said to Ketch, 'Prithee, let me feel the axe.' Touching the edge, he added, 'I fear it is not sharp enough.' To which Ketch replied, 'It is sharp and heavy enough.' It might well have been sharp and heavy in the right hands, but the first blow went wide of the mark, inflicting only a flesh wound and causing Monmouth to half raise himself and give the man a reproachful stare before resuming his position over the block. Worse was to follow, for a witness quoted in a contemporary pamphlet said, 'For all this the botcherly dog did so barbarously act his pairt that he could not at fyve stroakes of the ax sever the head from the body.' And the pamphlet continued, 'After the third stroke Ketch threw away the axe and offered forty guineas to anyone who would finish the work. The bystanders threatened to kill him unless he took up the axe again, and so he completed his task; if there had been no guard he would have been torn to pieces by the crowd.'

Before Monmouth's remains were finally interred in the Chapel Royal of St Peter ad Vincula within the Tower, the head was sewn on to the body again and a fine portrait of him, a scarf about his neck, was painted by the renowned artist Sir Godfrey Kneller, and is now displayed in the National Portrait Gallery in London.

## SEYMOUR, THOMAS, BARON SEYMOUR OF SUDELEY

Thomas Seymour, Baron and Lord Admiral, was born about 1508. He was a very ambitious and unscrupulous man and when Henry VIII died in 1547 he seized the opportunity to further his plans by marrying Henry's VIII's sixth wife, Queen Dowager Katherine Parr shortly afterwards. In a power struggle between himself and his elder brother, Edward, Duke of Somerset, he then attempted to turn his nephew, the ailing ten-year-old King Edward VI, against the Duke, who was acting as Regent and Protector, but failed to dislodge his rival.

Nothing daunted, he bided his time and, after the death of his wife on 5 September 1548, despite being suspected of having 'holpen her to her end', he turned his attentions to his ward, the young Princess Elizabeth, daughter of the late Anne Boleyn and then aged about fifteen.

But his machinations went too far and in January 1549 he was arrested. Despite threatening that 'whoever lays hands on me to fetch me to prison I shall thrust my dagger in him,' he was committed to the Tower. He faced no fewer than thirty charges, one being that he aspired to obtain the throne by attempting to gain an undue influence over his wife's step-daughter, the Princess Elizabeth, in order to persuade her to marry him. Evidence was given by the Princess's servants that Seymour had entered the royal bedroom in a state of undress and had 'tickled and played around with her', these allegations giving rise to further suspicions that the Princess was 'enceinte [pregnant] by the High Admiral'. Others stated that when she heard him coming, 'she ran out of hir bed to hir maydens and then went behynd the curteyns of hir bed'. And in the gardens at Hanworth, 'he wrated [romped] with hir and cut hir gowne in a hundred pieces, being black clothes'. Even when the Princess stayed with other noble families it was noted that 'the lady Elizabeth did bere some affection to the admiral, for some times she wolde blush if he were spoken of'.

On 27 February 1549 a Bill of Attainder was passed in Parliament sentencing him to death, the warrant being signed by the Regent; so much for brotherly love! The condemned man was taken to Tower Hill on the morning of 20 March 1549 and, while giving a last speech to the spectators, he was suddenly interrupted by 'an extraordinary and loud noise which affrighted all the people, so that many ran away or fell with terror to the ground; while others were thrust into the Tower moat'. At length a knight was seen riding towards the scaffold and the people, throwing up their hats, began to shout, 'A pardon, a pardon, God save the King!' But, far from bearing a reprieve, the horseman was the officer in charge of the train-band, the militia of Tower Hamlet, who had been ordered to report to the Lieutenant of the Tower, should he need more men to preserve the peace.

And so Thomas Seymour met his end. He died hard, for it was reported that he had a struggle, if not actually a stand-up fight with the executioner before he was overpowered and decapitated, two strokes of the axe being necessary, Archbishop Latimer later lamenting how the Baron had died 'very daungerously, yrksomelye, horryblye!' Following the execution his head and body were buried in the Tower's St Peter's Chapel, in accordance with an order issued by the Privy Council on 17 March.

As an interesting footnote (literally), the historian Strype said that when Seymour laid his head on the block he told his servant to 'speed the thing that he wot of'. On being interrogated the man confessed that his master was referring to two letters which he had written while in the Tower to the Lady Mary (Tudor, daughter of Catherine of Aragon, Henry's first wife) and to the Lady Elizabeth. Forbidden to communicate with anyone, the prisoner had used great ingenuity 'making ink so craftily that the like had not been seen before. He made his pen from the aglet [the metal tag of a lace] from a point he plucked from his hose. These two papers he then sewed between the sole of a velvet shoe he wore.'

The Protector and the Council quickly retrieved the dead man's shoes and found the concealed letters. Addressed to the two Princesses, each asserted that his brother the Regent was intent on depriving them of their right to the throne and urging them to do all in their power to bring about his downfall. But their efforts, if any, were not necessary, for two years later, having been found guilty on a charge of felony in planning to murder John Dudley, Earl of Warwick, who had supplanted him as Protector, Edward, Duke of Somerset was himself beheaded on Tower Hill.

## SPOTTISWOOD, SIR ROBERT

A talented and ambitious lawyer, Sir Robert was born in 1596 and studied at Oxford, later spending nine years in France, concentrating mainly on laws of theology. On returning to Scotland in June 1622, he was appointed a Privy Councillor by James VI and in the following month promoted to the Bench, taking the title Lord Newabbey. More success followed, Charles I favouring him with the appointment as President of a Court of Session, and when in 1634 John Elphinstone, 2nd Lord Balmerino, was accused of misprision of treason, Sir Robert was Crown Assessor.

Four years later, because of his opposition to the covenanters, those who believed that the Church should be governed by presbyters or elders, he sought refuge in England and, by 1643, had received the seals of office as Secretary of State from Charles I, one of the commissions he signed being that which appointed the Earl of Montrose (see Graham, James, p.101) as His Majesty's Lieutenant in Scotland. Sir Robert was with Montrose during the Battle of Philiphaugh on 13 September 1645 and was taken prisoner. Charged with having purchased the office of Secretary and also with conspiring with Montrose against the state, he was tried at St Andrews and although pleading that at Philiphaugh he had been unarmed and, moreover, had surrendered peaceably, he was sentenced to death. On 16 January 1646 he kept an appointment with the Scottish Maiden at the market cross at St Andrews.

# SQUIRE, EDWARD

A misguided and ill-fated man, Squire fell under the influence of Henry Walpole, a Jesuit priest of somewhat fanatical beliefs who felt that if a person's conversion to 'his' faith could not be achieved, the elimination of that person was the only answer, especially if that person was the Protestant Queen of England.

Walpole, born in 1558 and educated at Norwich and Cambridge, was intensely inspired by Edmund Campion, a Jesuit martyr, whose execution he witnessed at Tyburn in 1581. Three years later he joined the Jesuits on the Continent and, ordained priest in 1588, became a chaplain to the Spanish Army in Flanders in 1589–91.

About the same time Edward Squire, an under-groom in Queen Elizabeth's stables, left his employment to volunteer service with Sir Francis Drake's last expedition to the West Indies but the vessel he was in was captured by the Spanish and he was taken prisoner. In Spain he met Walpole, who promptly sought, and ultimately succeeded, to convert him to the Roman Catholic faith. So compliant was his pupil that the priest had little difficulty in convincing Squire that only the assassination of Queen Elizabeth could bring about the necessary radical change of religious beliefs in England. Squire, totally convinced, took an oath to carry out the deed; in modern parlance, he accepted the role of hitman.

The Jesuit priest had devised a bizarre plan whereby Squire, having access to the royal stables, would rub a toxic substance on the pommel of the Queen's saddle, and furthermore he supplied Squire with a quantity of the poison. He then arranged with the Spanish authorities to release their captive and allow him to return to England, at the same time promising the young man great reward and glory on the success of the mission.

When Squire reached this country he realized that he would need to make himself scarce after committing the foul deed, so he enlisted in an expedition being raised by Robert Devereux, the Queen's favourite, to fight the Spaniards in the Azores. Just before his departure he seized the opportunity to visit the stables and apply the toxic substance, then sailed with the expedition. On the voyage, obviously acting on Walpole's instructions, he likewise anointed Devereux's chair, but to his disappointment, the Earl's health remained unaffected.

Meanwhile, in 1593 Henry Walpole came to England to minister, illegally, to fellow Catholics, but was caught and arrested in Yorkshire. He was brought to the Tower where during the next two years he was racked several times but, with unimaginable courage, refused to divulge any information regarding his fellow Jesuits. However, doubtless convinced that his henchman had double-crossed him and that had the assassination taken place, he and other Catholics would by then have been able to practise their faith openly without fear of reprisal or torture, he informed his interrogators of Squire's treasonable intentions. Loyal to his faith and stubborn to the end, he was later taken to York where he was tried, found guilty and executed.

The hunt was now on for Edward Squire, but it was not until 1598 that he too was finally apprehended. Such was the efficacy of the Tower's persuasive devices that although initially denying everything, he soon yielded and, doubtless confronted with the fact that his late confessor had betrayed him, he admitted his guilt.

His trial was purely a formality, the official records stating that 'The ninth of November 1598, Edward Squire of Greenewich was arraigned at Westminster condemned of high Treason, and on the 13, drawne from the Tower to Tyborne and there hanged, bowelled and quartered.'

# STAFFORD, THOMAS

Born about 1531, the son of Lord Stafford, Thomas was one of the conspirators who with others (see Peckham, Henry, p.159) plotted to steal £50,000 from the Treasury with which to finance an uprising against Queen Mary. While some were caught and executed, he escaped with other companions to France but even from there he persisted in trying to overthrow the Queen. As Stow reported, 'there remaining in France diuuers times to stirre rebellion within this Realme by sending Bookes, Billes and Letters, written and printed, farced full of vntruthes, and at length the sayd Stafforde and other English rebels and some strangers, entred this Realm on the foure and twentieth of Aprill.'

Stafford, whose main object was said to have been to recover the long-lost title of the Duke of Buckingham, had mustered a small force of English, Scottish and French supporters and in a flotilla of only two ships, sailed from Dieppe. Landing on the Yorkshire coast he:

took by stealth the castle of Skarborough in the countie of Yorke and set out a shameful proclamation, wherein he traiterously called and affirmed the queene to be vnrightfull and most vnworthie queene, and forfeiting her crown by her marriage with a stranger [the King of Spain] who had brought into this realme the number of twelve thousand Spaniardes and that into their hands were delivered 12 of the strongest holdes in this Realme. In which proclamation the sayde Stafforde named himself Protector and gouernor of this Realme.

On word of this reaching London, little notice was taken of what was considered to be the ranting of a megalomaniac but, nevertheless, the Earl of Westmorland was ordered to take a large force of men just in case, and sort out the situation. This was achieved with little difficulty, for 'Stafforde, with other his complices, by the good diligence of the Earle of Westmerland and other noble men, were apprehended on the last of April.' All were taken into custody, Stafford being incarcerated in the Tower on 3 May 1557.

At his trial on 22 May he was charged with raising an insurrection and for stating his intention to depose Queen Mary and cast off the Spanish yoke. Six days later he was marched to Tower Hill where, according to the diarist Machyn, 'he was hanged on a cart, quartered, and so to Newgate to boil.' His head was spiked on London Bridge together with those of three of his fellow conspirators, Stretchley (or Strelly), Bradford and Procter, the latter trio having been hanged, drawn and quartered at Tyburn, and 'their sixteen quarters were sett up on every gatt in London'. Twenty-seven other rebels were tried and executed in Yorkshire for the same offence.

# STALEY, WILLIAM

In 1678 Titus Oates reported that many well-known Roman Catholic public figures were conspiring to overthrow Charles II and replace him with his brother the Duke of York (later James II). The religious frenzy that ensued swept the country and was further exacerbated by the mysterious and violent death of Sir Edmundbury Godfrey, the magistrate who had taken a statement on the subject from Oates. As a result of the 'Popish Plot', many celebrated heads rolled, those of Viscount Stafford and Dr Oliver Plunket among many others. One considerably less celebrated, at whom accusing fingers pointed, was William Staley, or Stayley, a Roman Catholic banker and goldsmith, who was accused of high treason, tried and found guilty.

The inevitable sentence, that he be hanged, drawn and quartered, was handed down by the judge, the grisly process duly taking place at Tyburn on 26 November 1678. However, his friends interceded on behalf of his relatives, pleading that his remains be given a decent burial rather than be exhibited, and this factor, supported by the fact that the condemned man had shown penitence during his trial, resulted in the concession being granted.

Accordingly, three days later, the burial service took place with great ceremony in St Paul's Church, Covent Garden. Alas, so ostentatious was the display of grief, so loud the Masses sung, that word of the funereal commotion reached the ears of the King – who promptly ordered that the grave be opened up, the dismembered and decapitated corpse be exhumed and the quarters displayed on the city's gates. Some fame, without doubt unsought and undesired, attached itself to Mr Staley, for his head, exhibited on London Bridge, was believed to have been the last to be spiked thereon.

## STONE, FATHER JOHN

Little is known of John Stone's earlier life other than that he became an Augustinian or Austin Friar. When, on 14 December 1538 the monks at the Canterbury house of that religious Order were required to sign the legal document acknowledging Henry VIII to be the recognized head of the Church in England, Friar Stone, a man of firm principles and unswerving devotion to his beliefs, was the only one among his fellow clerics to refuse to append his signature, declaring that, 'The King may not be head of the Church of England, it must be a spiritual father appointed by God.' Such defiance could have but one result; he was taken under escort to the Tower of London where he was confined until, on 27 October of the

187

following year, he was returned to Canterbury, there to be placed on trial charged with committing an offence under the 1535 Treason Act.

He was found guilty and sentenced to be hanged, drawn and quartered, his execution taking place on Saturday, 27 December 1539 just outside the city walls of Canterbury on Donjeon Hillock. The site was later renamed 'Dane John' as a lasting memorial to the courageous friar. Further recognition of his allegiance to his faith was forthcoming on 25 October 1970 when, together with thirty-nine other English martyrs, he was canonized.

On a more secular note, the bill for his execution, still held in the City Chamberlain's account book, shows the detailed cost of his execution:

| | |
|---|---:|
| Amount paid for half a tonne of timber to make a pair of gallowes for to hang ffryer stone | 2s.6d |
| For the cariage of the same tymber from Stablegate to the Dongeon | 4d |
| To a carpenter for makyng the same gallowes and the dray [cart] | 15d |
| To a laborer that dygged the holes | 3d |
| To four men to help sett vp the gallowes and for a drink for them | 8d |
| For a hardell [hurdle on which he was transported] | 6d |
| For a lode of wode and a hors to draw hym to the Dongeon | 2s.3d |
| For a halter to hang him | 1d |
| For two old halters [spares?] | 1d |
| To him that did the execyon | 4s.8d |
| To two men that set the ketill and parboyled hym | 12d |
| To a woman that scowred the kettyl | 2d |
| To three men that caryed his quarters to the gates and sett them vp | 12d |

Even in the sixteenth century, itemized bills were obviously demanded by the auditors.

## STORE, DOCTOR JOHN

As in any process, manufacturing or otherwise, modifications are always being introduced to improve the sequence of events, and so it was with Tyburn executions. The original method of transporting the victim from the gaol to the gallows was to have been dragged through the streets on a hurdle or cowhide, a procedure that meant only those in the front row of the crowds lining the route could see him or her. Moreover the flimsy conveyance provided such little protection against the bone-breaking cobbles that on many occasions the victim was found to be half dead on arrival, thereby depriving the impatiently waiting spectators of much of their entertainment. The solution was obvious – to use a cart instead. This had the added bonus that up to ten victims could be conveyed at any one time, all visible to the crowds en route. And, instead of the ladder which on arrival had to be scaled by the victim and twisted to one side to throw him off it after he had been noosed, the cart could be drawn up underneath the gallows, all the occupants could be noosed at the same time instead of one after the other, and a sharp slap on the horse's flank would bring about the cart's departure and so launch the passengers into eternity.

Similarly the very structure of the gallows itself was updated. Initially, criminals were hanged from the branches of the elm trees growing there but this primitive method was soon replaced by a permanent structure consisting of two uprights and a cross-piece known colloquially as the 'Tyburn Tree'. This design sufficed for many centuries, though it was inadequate when even greater numbers of victims were to be executed, so it was enlarged by the addition of a further upright and two cross-pieces, the resultant triangular shaped structure then being called the 'Triple Tree', capable of accommodating up to twenty-four occupants simultaneously. And just as a new ocean-going liner is launched by a celebrity so, on 1 June 1571, the first malefactor to be dispatched on the new model gallows was one who was considered distinctly worthy of that singular honour, Dr John Store.

But who was this man to be thus sentenced, and why was he so loathed that the public rejoiced? John Store, also known as Story, was born about 1510 and was educated at Oxford University. He became Bachelor of Civil Law in 1531, six years later being appointed principal of Broadgates Hall and created Doctor of Law. As a Justice of the Peace and Member of Parliament for Hindon in the early years of the reign of the Protestant King Edward VI, he made no attempt to conceal his fervent and dedicated support of the Roman Catholic faith; so forthright was he in fact that he was imprisoned by order of the House of Commons. On his release he fled to Flanders, where he remained until the throne was once again occupied by a devout Catholic, Queen Mary replacing Edward as the monarch. Confident of receiving support for his drastic opposition to Protestantism, he returned to England and quickly became renowned for his single-minded and savage persecution of Protestants, many of whom were put to death by being burned alive at the stake.

However, the religious pendulum swung once again when Queen Mary died in 1558, to be succeeded by her half-sister, the Protestant Elizabeth. Before two years had elapsed, Store had been arrested and confined in the Marshalsea Prison, London, but in 1563, with the connivance of the chaplain to the Spanish Ambassador, he escaped and made his way to the Continent. This time he obtained a lucrative post as a customs officer at Antwerp, where he was later alleged to have introduced the Spanish Inquisition on behalf of his patrons in Madrid, for which he received a pension granted by Philip II.

His very presence at the busy port not unnaturally antagonized the many English merchants coming ashore on business who recognized him, but it was not until August 1570 that the opportunity to exact retribution became feasible. Part of his duty was to inspect the cargoes of visiting ships and when he boarded one particular ship, owned by a Captain Parker, a carefully contrived plan was set in motion. As soon as his prey had descended the companionway into the hold, Parker promptly ordered the hatches to be nailed down, then hoisted sail and returned to England. The ship anchored at Yarmouth, its captain being greeted as a national hero by a rapturous public when news of his capture spread. *State Papers, Domestic* proclaimed: 'The locks and bolts of the Lollards' Tower [the Bishop of London's prison for heretics] were broken off at the death of Queen Mary and never since repaired. Now they were repaired for the reception of Dr Store.' But the captive was instead imprisoned in the Tower of London for many months, the accounts submitted by Sir Owen Hopton, Lieutenant of the Tower in respect of some of that time showing that: 'for the dyeot and chardges beginninge the 8 Aprill 1571 and ending the last of May, being in all 7 wekes and 5 days, at 13s. 4d the weke for himselfe, £5 3s. 4d; one keper (warder) at 5s. the weke 38s. 4d; fewell and candell at 4s. the weke, 30s. 7d; amounting to the sum of £8 12s. 3d.'

While confined there, Store was frequently interrogated and urged to take the oath of allegiance to Queen Elizabeth but, ever loyal to his principles and beliefs, he refused. Because he had lived in Spain at one time, the Spanish Ambassador in London attempted to intercede on the prisoner's behalf, whereupon the Queen allegedly retorted, 'The King of Spain may have his head if he wants it, but his body shall be left in England!'

Despite his advanced years – he was over sixty – Store was put on trial charged with committing high treason, 'for having consulted with one Prestal, a noted magician, against the Queen's life, for having conspired the death of her and the King of Scots, having cursed her in his grace at meals, and informed the Spanish how to invade England, raise a rebellion in Ireland and send the Scots into England.'

The outcome was inevitable for, found guilty, he was sentenced to be hanged, drawn and quartered, the penalty being exacted on 1 June 1571. It was one welcomed by the callous mob surrounding the Tyburn scaffold, for contemporary observers reported that, 'he was the object of general execration and care was taken that he should suffer all the torments of that horrible sentence.' That care certainly was taken was very much in evidence, for he was cut down while still alive and witnesses averred that 'the executioner slit open his stomach and while he was rifling through his bowels, Store sat up and dealt him a blow'. Decapitation and dismembering swiftly followed.

## STUART, JAMES IV OF SCOTLAND

A proud, capable and popular monarch, despite some opposition from some of his people, James maintained a truce with the English for seven long years, strengthening the ties by marrying Margaret, daughter of Henry VII. But three years after that King's death he signed a treaty with his country's old ally France, then at war with Henry VIII, even dispatching a fleet of warships to assist King Louis. It was then that he made the rash decision to take a more active role in the conflict and, leading a large Scottish army across the Border, he captured Norham Castle on the River Tweed and other strongholds, before pressing on southwards.

By 9 September 1513 his army had reached Flodden Field, south-east of the town of Coldstream, and there met the English forces under the Duke of Norfolk. Had he adopted a less reckless strategy and held his dominant position atop Flodden Hill, the outcome could have been less disastrous; as it was he led a charge to the plains below, failing to realize that by doing so, his enemy could, and did, outflank him and cut off any possible retreat back to the north. In the furious battle that followed, many brave Scots were killed, the forty-year-old King among them. And afterwards his corpse was found on the battlefield among the hundreds who were slain, and carried south by those who had crushed his troops and shattered his ambitions.

The body was taken to Sheen Monastery in Surrey, but let John Stow, Elizabethan historian, author of *Survey of London*, take up the story. Listing those interred in the Parish Church of St Michael in Wood Street, he continued:

Buried there is also the head of James, the fourth king of Scots of that name, slain at Flodden Field and buried here on this occasion [i.e. the reason being]; after the battle the body of the said king being found, was enclosed in lead and conveyed from thence to London and so to the monastery of Sheen in Surrey, where it remained for a time, in what order I am not certain. But since the dissolution of that holy place in the reign of Edward VI, Henry Grey, Duke of Suffolk living there, I have been shown the same body so lapped in lead close [tightly] to the head and body, thrown into a waste room among the old timber, lead, and other rubble. Since the which time, workmen there, for their foolish pleasure, hewed off his head, and Launcelot Young, master glazier to her majesty [Queen Elizabeth], feeling a sweet savour to come from it and seeing the same dried from all the moisture and yet its form remaining, with the hair on its head and beard red, brought it from there to his house in Wood Street, London, where for a time he kept it for the sweetness, but in the end caused the sexton of that church to bury it among other bones taken out of their charnel.

There can be but few monarchs without a suitable monument on their graves, but alas at his burial, James IV was even denied that.

## STUART, MARY, QUEEN OF SCOTS

B orn at Linlithgow, Scotland on 8 December 1542, Mary Stuart was the daughter of James V of Scotland and the great-granddaughter of Henry VII. From the age of five the Princess Mary was brought up in France where she was betrothed to the Dauphin, Francis. They married when she was sixteen, he a year younger, but when he died prematurely she returned to Scotland to find the country largely Protestant, many being hostile to her Catholic beliefs and upbringing. Mary was an attractive and vivacious woman and the years that followed were emotionally turbulent. After she had been forced to abdicate from the Scottish throne by her Protestant opponents, she sought refuge in England in 1568, only to be accused by Queen Elizabeth of complicity in the brutal murder of Darnley, her second husband, and imprisoned in Tutbury Castle.

Although she had lost her freedom, many plots were subsequently uncovered, various factions seeking to re-establish her on the Scottish throne, to enlist Spanish aid and invade England, to overthrow Elizabeth and restore Catholicism to England. A letter was discovered, allegedly written by Mary, discussing the possibility of Elizabeth's assassination, and although initially reluctant to take drastic action against her kinswoman, Elizabeth eventually decided that the threat was too dire to ignore. On 26 September 1586 Mary was brought as a state prisoner to Fotheringhay Castle, near Peterborough, Northamptonshire (now, regrettably, a ruin) and in the month following she was accused of having engaged in treasonable correspondence, and after being tried by the Court of Star Chamber she was sentenced to death.

On 8 February 1587 Mary, Queen of Scots was executed within Fotheringhay Castle, a rare, if not the only occasion, on which a judicial beheading had been performed within a building. The reason for this could well have been for security purposes, to prevent any violent demonstrations, for only official witnesses were allowed to be present.

In the Great Hall a scaffold had been erected, two feet high and twelve feet long with rails around its edges, draped with black cloth, and there, in the presence of the Earls of Kent and Shrewsbury together with officers of the court and Church dignitaries, the Queen sat on a low stool, appearing calm and composed as the warrant for her execution was read out. Then her ladies-in-waiting prepared her for her ordeal. As they removed her black robes she was seen to be wearing a red velvet petticoat and silk scarlet bodice. Taking off the petticoat, she donned a pair of scarlet satin sleeves over her kirtle (dress), exclaiming indignantly as she did so that 'she had never seen grooms to make her unready, and that she had never put off her clothes in such a company!'

A hassock had been placed in front of the block, and kneeling on it, Mary held her beads and a crucifix as she prayed. The executioner, a man named Simon Bull, then knelt and begged her forgiveness, to which she replied, 'I forgive you with all my heart for now I hope you shall make an end of all my troubles.' One of her women then took a Corpus Christi cloth and, folding it in a triangular shape, secured it so that it covered her eyes, moving to one side as her mistress positioned her neck on the block. Bull, on seeing her attempt to cushion her neck on the hard surface with her hands, signalled his assistant, described as 'the bloody and unseemly varlet attending upon him', to move them to her sides, lest her arms deflect his aim. But, doubtless overwhelmed by being the cynosure of all eyes and the fact that he was about to kill a queen, his first blow went awry, the axe striking the knot of her blindfold at the back of her head and mercifully stunning her. His second blow was more accurate, virtually severing her head although a little gristle required him to use his knife.

It was reported that 'Mary's dressing of lawn [a cloth of fine linen or cotton] then falling from her head, her hair appeared as grey as one of three-score-and-ten years old, polled very short, her face being so much altered from the form she had when she was alive, as few could remember by her face.' Then the executioner, taking hold of the head probably between his hands, held it high and gave the traditional, though under the circumstances, macabre proclamation, 'God save the Queen!' referring of course to Elizabeth, not to the Queen he had just decapitated.

The report continued:

Her lips stirred up and down a quarter of an hour after her head was cut off. Then one of the executioners espied her little dog which had crept under her clothes, which could not be gotten forth but by force, yet afterwards would not depart from the dead corpse but came and lay between her head and her shoulders, which being imbrued with her blood, it was carried away and washed. And all things else that had any blood were either burned or clean washed, and the executioners went away with money for their fees, not having any one thing that belonged unto her.

The latter precaution was doubtless to prevent the acquisition of anything that could be later venerated as a holy relic, although in March 1999 a lock of her hair was one of the many items to be auctioned which had belonged to the late Marchioness of Dufferin and Ava, its estimate being £2000–£3000; as Mary had her hair 'polled very short', it is likely that the lock of hair in question was obtained during her earlier years.

Following the decapitation it was necessary to avoid any later accusations that the authorities had an ulterior motive for holding the execution in private, perhaps someone other than the Queen being executed, and so, as proof, the severed head was washed and placed on a cushion in the window bay, outside which a large crowd had gathered. After being left on display for some little time, the head and the body were taken to an upper room, there to be embalmed by surgeons. This procedure was essential, for about six months elapsed before her burial at Peterborough on 1 August 1587, the gravedigger being Old Scarlett, a sturdy, bearded fellow who, it was reported, had also buried Queen Catherine of Aragon.

It was not until 1613 that her son James I had the body-shaped coffin exhumed and brought south in a hearse drawn by six black horses and escorted by many noblemen. Passing along the 'Reading Road' – now Piccadilly – via Charing Cross to Westminster Abbey, there it was deposited in a vault within the Henry the Seventh Chapel. Mary was a tall woman, six feet in height and, her head having been positioned once more on her shoulders, the leaden coffin is, with the exception of that of her great-grandfather Henry VII, the longest in the Abbey.

## THISTLEWOOD, ARTHUR
## BRUNT, JOHN
## TIDD, RICHARD
## INGS, JAMES
## DAVIDSON, WILLIAM

Had the plans concocted by these desperadoes in a house in Cato Street, since renamed Homer Street, near the Edgware Road in London, been successful, they would have assassinated members of the Cabinet, seized the Mansion House and the Bank of England, using arms stolen from a gunsmith's shop and six cannon from the artillery grounds for which they had ammunition, and taken over the Tower of London. Their leader, Arthur Thistlewood, spendthrift, revolutionary and born agitator, had discovered the date on which many of the Government ministers would be dining with Lord Harrowby at his house, 39 Grosvenor Square, and together with his fellow conspirators, decided that the first part of his plan would be to burst in and massacre them all. Fortunately for the Cabinet members – but not for the gang – prior information was leaked to the authorities by one of the conspirators named John Monument who turned King's evidence. The police promptly raided their meeting place and arrested them, their leader later being captured at No. 8 White Street, Little Moorfields. And on 3 March 1820 they at least achieved the last part of their plan by entering the Tower of London – but as prisoners.

At their subsequent trial all were found guilty of treason but the nineteenth century, being rather more civilized than earlier ones, the usual death sentence for treason, that of being hanged, drawn and quartered, had been somewhat ameliorated by the exclusion of the ghastly 'disembowelling while still alive' surgical operation. So the sentence passed by the Lord Chief Justice Abbott (no relation!) stated:

> That you and each of you be taken from hence to the gaol from whence you came, and from thence that you be drawn upon a hurdle to the place of execution and there be hanged by the neck until you be dead; and that afterwards your heads shall be severed from your bodies, and your bodies divided into four quarters, to be disposed of as His Majesty shall think fit. And may God of His infinite goodness have mercy upon your souls.

The executions were planned to take place on 1st May 1820 on the public scaffold outside Newgate Prison (where the Old Bailey Central Criminal Court now stands), the platform itself having to be enlarged by a further ten feet to allow more space for the decapitations to be performed. Such was the intense publicity and the expectation by the authorities of vast numbers of spectators attending, that double rows of railings were erected across Giltspur, Newgate and Skinner Streets, and all other approaches to the prison. Positions in the windows of adjacent streets commanding a good view of the scaffold were being hired out at prices which, although outrageously exorbitant, did little to deter would-be customers. Troops were called in to control the crowds who flocked to the area during the night and the Lord Mayor prepared himself to read the Riot Act, the declaration which would virtually bring martial law into effect if matters got out of hand. Soon after 5 am sawdust was strewn across the scaffold boards and black cloth draped as a backdrop behind the gallows, heightening the macabre scene. At 7 am the London executioner, James Botting, a man not known for his gentle sensitivity, made his appearance to position the steps by which he would secure the hanging ropes to the crossbeam. Next, five empty coffins were brought out and placed in readiness by the scaffold, the workmen throwing sawdust into them to prevent the blood soaking through the wood. The tension really started to mount when the block was brought out and placed at the head of the first coffin, its shape bringing murmurs of surprise from the know-alls in the crowd, for instead of being flat-topped, it had been carved so that the top presented a sharp edge.

Then the condemned men appeared through the prison doorway. Thistlewood led, his face pale, his demeanour calm and without bravado as he held out his wrists for James Foxen, the assistant hangman, to bind them. Tidd was next to appear, smiling and chatting cheerfully to the turnkey as the man started to drive the rivets out of the irons encircling the prisoner's ankles. Once free, Tidd ran across to Thistlewood and, shaking hands with him, exclaimed, 'Well, Mr Thistlewood, how do you do?' Each had been given an orange, doubtless to alleviate their inevitably dry throats, and Tidd sucked his as they chatted. Next came Ings, all eyes on him as he danced along to join the others. He was dressed in his working clothes, those of a butcher, with a rough pepper-and-salt jacket and a dirty cap. Obviously under considerable stress, he laughed and shouted as his irons were being removed. He was closely followed by Brunt, who remained perfectly composed while being prepared for the ordeal, only saying to his companions, 'All will soon be well.' The last man, Davidson, arrived, his lips moving in silent prayer, to take his place on the bench alongside the others.

With the arrival of the chaplain, the first procession set off, the cleric and officials leading Thistlewood up on to the scaffold. There the cap was placed on his head but in response to his request, it was not pulled down over his eyes. Botting placed the noose around the prisoner's neck and signalled that the others should be brought up one at a time to be similarly capped and noosed. Tidd was next, tripping as he mounted the steps but recovering his balance, and was greeted with loud cheers from the crowd, many of whom would not have been unduly upset had the Government been removed, albeit in a less bloodthirsty manner. He continued to suck his orange as he co-operated with Botting in the positioning of the noose and he too preferred to see what was to befall him and his companions.

Ings, still gripped by high emotions, bounded on to the platform, exclaiming to the hangman, 'Now, old man, finish me tidily, tie the handkerchief tight over my eyes; pull the noose tighter, it may slip'. Davidson joined him, bowed to the crowd, then submitted to being blindfolded and noosed. Lastly Brunt, who was by now so hyped up that he took a pinch of snuff from a piece of paper he held in his hand and followed this by kicking off his shoes.

All was ready. Mr Cotton, the chaplain, began to read the final prayers and even as he did so, Botting operated the trap, the five falling but a few feet and still in full view of the spectators who stared hypnotized as Thistlewood was seen to struggle only slightly, whereas Ings jerked so convulsively that the assistant hangman, Foxen, had to pull on his legs for nearly five minutes before the body swung inertly.

The attitude of some of the spectators that day was described by the author of the *Journal of Mrs Arbuthnot*, published March 1820:

My brother Cecil, who has never seen an execution, told me he had a great curiosity on this occasion and went. He wished very much to see how they would behave, but when they were tied up, he felt so nervous and in fact felt so much more than they did themselves that he retired into the corner of the specially hired room and hid himself, that he might not see the drop fall, which excited great contempt in the people who were in the room with him; among whom was one woman, young and pretty and very decent looking, who kept her eyes fixed on it all the time and, when they had hung a few seconds, exclaimed, 'There's two on them not dead yet!'

Half an hour passed before Botting resumed his grim task, first lifting each pendant cadaver into a sitting position, propping their feet on the edge of the drop, then raising the trapdoors so his assistant could stand on them and hold each corpse while the hangman cut the ropes. Thistlewood was the first, his body being lowered into the coffin with his neck positioned on the sharp edged block. The noose and cap were taken off, the removal of the latter revealing the face purple with suffused blood. The coat and waistcoat were drawn down by Foxen, exposing the neck, and although an axe lay on the scaffold, the man who then approached held in his hand a small, surgical-type knife. The stranger wore a blue jacket and dark grey trousers; his hat was pulled low and his features were hidden behind a mask which extended over his mouth. Bending over the corpse, he deftly severed the head and handed it to Foxen, who then held it high and delivered the traditional proclamation 'This is the head of Arthur Thistlewood, the traitor!' his voice being barely audible above the groans, the hooting and hissing that rose from the crowd. The torso was then drawn down into the coffin and the head replaced on the shoulders.

The block was moved along to the next coffin and the same ghastly ceremony repeated a further four times, the masked man having to replace his blunted knife at least twice. As the last head was held high, the now volatile crowd erupted into violence and Botting and Foxen had to flee for their very lives behind Newgate's massive gates. After some order had been restored by the hundreds of constables and soldiers, quicklime was poured over the corpses and the coffins were taken back into the prison, there to be buried in unmarked graves. And with the demise of the Cato Street conspirators, the reign of the heading axe, the cleaver and ripping knife finally came to an end.

## TOUCHET, MERVYN, LORD AUDLEY, 2nd EARL OF CASTLEHAVEN

Had tabloid newspapers been invented three hundred or so years earlier, their editors would have exulted at the scandal uncovered by their investigative journalists and their front pages would have carried banner headlines, though doubtless the seventeenth-century scribes who sold their broadsheets and tracts on London's streets in 1631 did not overlook this spicy piece of gossip. For Mervyn Touchet, Lord Audley of Hely or Heligh, of Fonthill Gifford near Shaftesbury in Wiltshire, was not only eccentric but had committed several almost unmentionable crimes, not the least of which was the rape of his wife.

Upon the offences being reported by Lady Audley and her eldest son James, Mervyn was arrested and put on trial, not in the House of Lords as was the custom, but at the Lent Assizes held in his home county of Wiltshire, there to face twenty-seven Lord Triers (those appointed to try the case) and eight Judges, presided over by the Lord High Steward. During that trial several important points of law were established, one being that a peer of the realm could not be tried by a common jury but only by his fellow peers; that a peer could not challenge any of his peers or have counsel, defence barristers etc, except on points of law. That contrary to the usual practice, a wife could give evidence against her husband if it was a case of rape and she was the party wronged; and finally, that 'if a Man took a maid by Force and ravished her, and she afterwards gave her Consent, and married him, this would not purge the Offence, but it was still a Rape.'

Having got all that clear, the trial started, Lady Audley giving evidence that on the second night of their marriage her husband had invited a man named Ampthill into the bedroom and encouraged him to embrace her. What made it even more shocking was that Ampthill had been a former page-boy of the household but was now a relative of the family, Mervyn having forced his daughter by an earlier marriage to marry him.

Nor was that all, for Her Ladyship testified that on another occasion she was asleep and woke up to find her husband and a servant called Brodway in the room. Resist as she might, surrender was inevitable, for her husband held both her hands and one of her legs 'till Brodway lay with her'. By now reduced to tears in the courtroom, she described how she had seized a knife, intending to kill herself, but that Brodway had forced it from her grasp. More disgraceful revelations were to follow, another servant, Skipworth, stating that his master 'had made him lie with the young Lady Audley, the wife of his son, a girl who was but twelve years old.'

Rumours abounded locally to the effect that Lady Audley was far from being the innocent and unsullied lady she professed to be, but that once the 'assaults' became public knowledge, probably through gossip by the servants, she had to bring charges in order to protect her reputation. Also her eldest son James could well have had ulterior motives in supporting the charges she had made, a likely one being his ambition to succeed to his father's title.

In addition to those charges against His Lordship, others alleging sodomy with various of his servants were also considered by the court. After lengthy deliberation the Lord Triers returned a unanimous verdict of not guilty on the homosexual charges but found Mervyn Touchet guilty of rape.

He was deprived of his title as Baron Audley of Hely (his son James regaining it two years later) and was sentenced to be hanged, but in view of his noble birth, 'he obtained the favour of being beheaded'.

Awaiting execution in the Tower, he received spiritual solace daily, administered by the Dean of St Paul's, and on 14 May 1631 was beheaded on Tower Hill, exhibiting to the vast crowd of scaffold afficionados 'a very manly and cheerful countenance such as seemed no wise daunted by the fear of death'.

As an object lesson demonstrating the inadvisability of acting as a defence witness, it was reported that two of the three servants who gave evidence in court against Mervyn Touchet were themselves later brought to trial, doubtless for 'assaulting and having carnal knowledge of Lady Audley', if nothing more serious. They were found guilty and executed. Being commoners and thereby undeserving of the favour enjoyed by their master, they were, of course, hanged.

## TOWNELEY, COLONEL FRANCIS

Nowadays, office workers and tourists walking along Fleet Street have no particular reason to raise their eyes higher than usual, but this was far from the case in the seventeenth and eighteenth centuries when the stone archway, Temple Bar, straddled that roadway, for those passers-by unable to resist the temptation to glance upwards would find themselves looking into the sightless eyes of the heads which adorned that structure. And the last head to be exhibited thereon was that of Colonel Francis Towneley, severed, coincidentally, by John Thrift, the last executioner to dispatch his victims by the axe.

Towneley was born at Towneley Hall, Lancashire, in 1709, a member of the Roman Catholic faith who, despite being of English descent, was a fervent supporter of the Stuart cause, doubtless inspired by the example set by his Uncle Richard who, in 1715, had fought with the Jacobites. At the age of nineteen Francis went to France and on meeting other Jacobites exiled in that country was further encouraged by being introduced to Charles Edward, Bonnie Prince Charles. The French King Louis, impressed by the young man's martial potential, granted him a commission in the army, Towneley proving his mettle at the Siege of Phillipsburgh in 1733 before returning to England where, the political plot and counterplot being at fever pitch, he joined Charles Edward's Highlanders and with them marched south over the border. Carlisle was captured, Penrith, Lancaster and Preston also falling under their assault for although their forces numbered only 4500 men they met little resistance. Maintaining their impetus they approached Manchester, that city being captured, it was said at the time 'by a drummer and a whore marching ahead even of the advance guard, to enlist more recruits'! However, only two hundred or so joined and these, together with a few other Englishmen, were formed into the Manchester Regiment and placed under the command of Francis Towneley, now promoted Colonel.

But as they continued south towards Derby, word came that the notorious Duke of Cumberland (known as the 'Butcher' by the Scots but so admired by his supporters that the flower 'Sweet William' was named after him) was advancing with an army twice the size of the Scots'; other troops were being assembled to defend London. And so the Prince turned back towards the border. On reaching Carlisle once more, albeit from the opposite direction, Towneley, his much depleted regiment now consisting of but 114 soldiers and 250 Highlanders of the Duke of Perth's Regiment, was given the hopeless task of holding that city while the rest of the Scottish army continued their headlong retreat into Scotland. Two days later Cumberland's army arrived, bringing with it heavy artillery; Towneley, desperately short of supplies and with no hope of reinforcements, urged that the garrison be allowed to fight their way out but the city's governor overruled him and surrendered on 30 December 1745, on condition 'that they were not to be put to the sword but be held at the King's Pleasure'. The surrender was accepted but the plea callously disregarded, the Duke of Cumberland exclaiming, 'I wish I could have blooded my soldiers with those villains [the Carlisle defenders] but it would have cost us many a brave fellow, and it comes to the same end, as they will have no sort of claim on the King's mercy and I sincerely hope they will meet with none.'

His words were prophetic, for at Colonel Towneley's trial in the Court House at St Margaret's Hill, London in June 1746, he was charged with committing high treason, found guilty and condemned to be hanged, drawn and quartered, George II showing that the 'King's Pleasure' amounted to no more than that of confirmation of the sentence. On 20 July following, he and George Fletcher, a fellow Jacobite officer, were dragged, each on a hurdle, from New Gaol, Southwark to the gallows on Kennington Common where the ghastly executions were performed. Francis Towneley's ordeal at Thrift's unsteady hands was described in the relevant *State Trials*:

> After he had hung six minutes he was cut down and, having life in him as he lay on the block to be quartered, the executioner gave him several blows to his breast, which not having the effect designed, he immediately cut his throat; after which he took his head off, then ripped him open and took out his bowels and heart and threw them in a fire which consumed them. Then he slashed his four quarters and put them with the head into a coffin, and they were carried back to the gaol from whence he came, and on 2 August 1746 the head was put on Temple Bar and his body and limbs suffered to be buried.

Together with that of Fletcher, Towneley's head was duly displayed to the crowds flocking to Fleet Street. Public interest in the fate of the defeated Scottish leaders was intense, posters being distributed and broadsheet ballads sold, extolling England's victory over the Scots. Horace Walpole wrote to a friend on 16 August 1746 describing how, on his way to visit the Tower of London, 'while passing under the new heads at Temple Bar, I saw people making a trade of letting [hiring] spy-glasses at a halfpenny a look.'

The heads remained there for the next twenty-six years,

although they were nearly dislodged when, as reported in the *Annual Register*, on 20 January 1766 a man was arrested and charged with having fired musket balls from a crossbow at the two heads at 2.30 in the morning. In court not only did he seek to justify his actions by asserting that the two Jacobites had not been punished enough already, but boasted that he had also peppered them with shot on the three previous nights and, moreover, had intended to continue the fusillade until he had fired the fifty musket balls found in his possession.

During a gale on 1 April 1772 one head fell to the ground, followed by the other, causing understandable havoc among passers-by for, while one could get accustomed to and even ignore the grim trophies positioned on high, the effect of seeing them at close range was, to say the least, revolting. As summed up by the wife of the editor of the contemporary *Morning Chronicle*, 'When the black, shapeless lump fell, women screamed and men gasped in horror. One woman near me fainted at the ghastly sight!'

When the news reached Towneley Hall, a family retainer journeyed south and probably by surreptitious means, succeeded in gaining possession of his late master's head. He then brought it back to the Hall, its arrival home doubtless greeted with mingled sorrow and heartfelt relief at its retrieval. For years the relic was then kept in a large basket covered with a napkin in the Red drawing room, but eventually it was deposited in a small cupboard in the oak panelling of the family chapel. When finally it was decided to bring it out into the light of day, the deleterious effect of adjacent hot-water pipes became apparent, for its remaining hair was now crinkly and brittle, the skull and teeth blackened. In order to protect it in the future it was sealed in a glass box, supported by small pieces of oak from the Towneley estate, and buried beneath the chapel's altar.

When the Hall became the property of Burnley Corporation

in 1900 and transformed into a superb museum and art gallery, the Towneley possessions, including the precious relic of course, were removed and retained by the family. On 12 August 1947 it was decided by Maurice Towneley-O'Hagan, 3rd Baron O'Hagan, that as far as possible the head should be given the equivalent of a Christian burial; accordingly it was interred in the tomb on the south side of the Towneley Chapel in St Peter's Parish Church, Burnley, a final and fitting resting-place for a brave and loyal soldier who gave his life for his Cause.

## TUDOR, OWEN

A Welshman of distinguished Anglesey lineage, Owen Tudor was appointed to the court of Henry V as a page, and although somewhat later he became 'a common soldier with an income of less than £40 a year', his sterling service on the battlefield at Agincourt gained him promotion as a Squire of the Body to the King. When Henry V died in 1422, Owen was appointed Clerk to the Wardrobe to the Dowager Queen Katherine de Valois and so continued to move in court circles. Being, it was said, 'a giant in stature and as handsome as Mars', he made a considerable impact in more ways than one, on the young woman, for on one festive occasion, as reported by contemporary royal watchers, Owen was urged to dance in front of her and, while attempting an over-ambitious pirouette, lost his balance and fell, finishing up with his head in the royal lap.

This intimate, albeit accidental, encounter was instrumental in furthering a close personal relationship between them, so close indeed that the ladies of the court remarked unfavourably on the Queen's behaviour, reproving her for 'lowering herself in paying any attention to a person who, though possessing some personal accomplishments and advantages, yet had no princely or even gentle alliance, but belonging to a barbarous class of savages inferior to the lowest English yeoman.' To which unacceptable criticism Her Majesty retorted that, 'being a Frenchwoman she had not been aware that there was any difference of race in the British island.'

Their romance blossomed and they clandestinely married in about 1425, five children, three sons and two daughters, being born to the socially ill-assorted couple. Despite this, the union was kept surprisingly secret for many years, but when Humphrey, Duke of Gloucester, who was Regent during the young King Henry VI's minority, found out, his reactions were as violent as could be expected, since he perceived that a son of such a marriage might well pose a challenge to the present King, who was, after all, only Owen's stepson. In a belated attempt to destroy such a threat he drafted a statute warning that 'anyone who should dare to marry a Queen-Dowager, or any lady holding lands of the Crown, without the consent of the King and Council would suffer the severest penalties.'

Although this statute never became law, Queen Katherine had no option but to move into royal lodgings at the Priory in Bermondsey where, in 1437, she died, sadly only thirty-six years old. At that, Gloucester issued a summons in the name of the young King stating that, 'His Majesty wills that Owen Tudor, who had dwelt with his mother, should come into his presence.' But, wary of the Regent's motives, Owen Tudor sought sanctuary in Westminster Abbey, only giving himself up when the Regent promised him safe passage back to Wales. However, having avoided one trap, the Welshman walked into another one set by the Earl of Suffolk who, doubtless at Gloucester's instigation, had him imprisoned in Wallingford Castle.

Some time later he was transferred to Newgate Prison from where, ever a man of action, he escaped from his cell and on being recaptured was confined in the Tower of London. It was probably then realized by the authorities that, despite having married a queen, he was, after all, still a commoner, and so did not qualify for accommodation in the State Prison – and back he went to Newgate!

Again he managed to get away from that gaol, as reported in an anonymous manuscript:

> This same yere, 22 Henry VI [1444] one Oweyn, no man of birthe neither of livelihood, brak out of Newgate at night at serchynge tyme through help of his priest and wente his way, hurtyinge foule his keeper, but at the last, blessyd be God, he was taken agane, the whiche Oweyn hadd prevylie [privately] wedded the Quene Katherine and had ii or iii chyldren by her, unwetying [unknown to] the commin people tyl that she were dyed and buryed.

When Henry VI came of age, Owen found himself back in the royal favour for the King ordered his release from prison and not only granted him an annuity but in 1460 appointed him King's Lieutenant of Denbighshire, its royal parks being extensive areas of fertile countryside grazed by numerous herds of fallow deer.

On the outbreak of the Wars of the Roses he was given a captaincy in the Lancastrian forces and the army, under the command of one of his sons, Jasper, pursued the Earl of March towards the Welsh borders. However, on reaching Mortimer's Cross between Wigmore and Leominster, on 2 February 1461, their opponents turned at bay, a fierce battle raging until dusk. Jasper Tudor conducted a tactical withdrawal but Owen, with true Welsh tenacity and courage, refused to retreat and was captured.

He was taken to Hereford, where he was sentenced to be beheaded in that city's market square. Until the very last moment, he fervently believed that he would be reprieved, as reported by a contemporary historian: 'He waved all away and trusted he would not be beheaded, until he saw the axe and the block, and he still trusted on pardon and grace until the collar of his red velvet doublet was ripped off. Then he said, "This head shall lie on the block that was wont to lie on Queen Katherine's lap" and put his heart and mind wholly unto God and full meekly took his death.' It was also recorded that after the decapitation, the head was, in accordance with custom, placed on the market cross whereupon, 'A woman among the crowd carefully combed his hair and washed away the blood off his face and she got candles and set them about his head.'

His remains were buried within the Priory of Grey Friars in Hereford and when, during the late 1800s, pipelines were laid to supply gas to residences near the river, the excavations caused the foundations of the Priory to be exposed, these being between the River Wye and another church, that of St Nicholas. On 24 October 1933 workmen digging a drainage trench on the site of that long-demolished place of worship discovered three skeletons buried three feet down in the ground. One skeleton was that of a man six feet two inches tall, and so was considered to be that of Owen Tudor, 'a giant in stature'. His remains were reinterred nearby, but without the honours and glory which should have accompanied the burial, for Owen Tudor was none other than the founder of the Tudor dynasty, his eldest son Edmund by Katherine de Valois becoming Earl of Richmond, father of Henry VII, the line continuing through Henry VIII and Queens Mary and Elizabeth.

Venturing along the 'what if' trail, one wonders what would have happened had Owen been killed at Agincourt, or had maintained his balance in the pirouette – in other words, if he had never married Katherine? Then there would have been no all-powerful Tudor dynasty; no Henry VII, no Henry VIII – so Anne Boleyn, Katherine Howard, Archbishop Fisher and Sir

Thomas More among many others would have retained their heads; no Queen Mary, Henry's daughter by Catherine of Aragon – so no execution by the axe for Lady Jane Grey, her husband, Lord Guildford Dudley or her father the Duke of Suffolk; no burnings of countless Protestant martyrs; Elizabeth, Henry's daughter by Anne Boleyn, would not have been born – and many Catholic priests would have continued to practise their faith into ripe old age. But who knows – perhaps worse, far worse monarchs might have ruled instead.

# TYRELL, SIR JAMES

Sir James was a dedicated Yorkist and was knighted after the Battle of Tewkesbury in 1471, six years later becoming Member of Parliament for Cornwall. A strong supporter of the Duke of Gloucester (later Richard III), he is believed by many to have been the Duke's hit man, smoothing his master's path to the throne by eliminating those juvenile obstacles, the Little Princes held in the Tower.

In his remarkable book *Historie of Kyng Rycharde the Thirde* written about 1513, Sir Thomas More described the likely train of events which took place, and what happened to the two boys, accounts probably received from Cardinal Morton, Bishop of Ely, who was in a position to know the facts and in whose household he was brought up. First explaining how Richard III, at that time believed to have been at Warwick, dispatched Sir James Tyrell, his Master of Horse, with a letter to the Constable of the Tower, Sir Robert Brackenbury, ordering him to deliver up the keys of that castle to the bearer for one night, Sir Thomas described how Tyrell took possession and directed Miles Forrest, one of the Princes' attendants, 'a felowe fleshed in murther before time' and John Dighton 'a big brode square strong knaue', to smother them in their sleep. These two 'about midnight, the sely children lying in their beddes, came into the chamber and sodainly lapped them vp among the clothes, so bewrapped them and entangled them, keping down by force the fetherbed and pillowes hard vnto their mouthes, that within a while smored and stifled, thyr breath failing, thei gaue vp to God their innocent soules.'

The murderers then called in Tyrell who 'vpon the sight of them, caused those two murtherers to burye them at the stayre foote, metely depe in the grounde vnder a great heape of stones.' Tyrell then rode off to King Richard who 'gaue hym gret thanks'. For the heinous crime, ringleader Tyrell was amply rewarded, being appointed steward of the Duchy of Cornwall and Chamberlain of the Exchequer. Following the death of Richard III on the battlefield at Bosworth in 1485, Sir James was given the post of Governor of the Castle and Town of Guisnes near Calais in 1486. He may well have been suspected of complicity in the murders but, the two small corpses not having been discovered (but see my *Mysteries of the Tower of London*), evidence was not forthcoming. However his fortunes changed dramatically when in May 1502 he was accused of aiding a political prisoner, Edmund de la Pole, to escape from prison, and also of offering to surrender Guisnes Castle to the French. When charged with high treason for those offences, he is also believed to have confessed to the murder of the two Princes, Sir Thomas More stating: 'Very trouthe is it and well knowen that at such a time as syr James Tirell was in the Tower for Treason committed agaynste the moste famous Prince King Henry the seuenth (in May 1502) bothe Dighton and he were examined and confessed the murther in maner aboue writen.' And the *Great Chronicle of London* repeated those details, saying: 'Concideryng the deth of Kyng Edwardys chyldyr Of whom as men feared not opynly to saye, that they were rydd owth of this world . . . of which cruell dede Sr Jamys Tyrell was Reportid to be the doer . . .'

And whether he climbed the spiral stairs of the Bloody Tower that night in 1483 or not, one fact is indisputable: on 6 May 1502 he certainly mounted the scaffold steps on Tower Hill and paid the ultimate price, his severed head and body then being buried in Augustine Friars Church.

# WALLACE, SIR WILLIAM

In 1296 Edward I was determined to crush Scottish opposition and, after showing little mercy to the inhabitants of Berwick, returned to England, taking with him the Stone of Scone on which Scottish kings had been crowned since time immemorial. He left behind him a country apparently submissive, English garrisons under the command of the Earl of Surrey and his treasurer Cressingham being strategically stationed to put down any unrest. But the Scots were far from quelled and the more vehement and determined among them mobilized under the leadership of Sir William Wallace, a descendant of a noble family in Clydedale. And in May 1297 they attacked Lanark, slaying Sir William Hezelrig, Sheriff of that town and, continuing their triumphant advance, not only forced the English to flee from Perth but, by September, even laid siege to the heavily defended castles of Dundee and Stirling.

At the latter city, Sir William's forces met Surrey's army in battle and, gaining a commanding position at the foot of the Abbey Crag, atop which was later erected a national monument to his proud memory, Wallace and his men isolated and defeated those of the enemy who had crossed the wooden bridge over the Forth. Decimated and demoralized, the rest of the English army fled, a further blow being struck against the English overlords when the profligate Cressingham was killed, his skin then tanned for use as sword belts. Raids across the border followed, towns and isolated farms in Northumberland, Cumberland and Westmorland being attacked, their horses and cattle stolen, their houses burned.

Having restored honour to the Scots by expelling the 'invaders' from their country, Sir William was elected Governor of Scotland, but his victory was to be short-lived for at this challenge to his authority, King Edward raised an army numbering nearly 90,000 men and in July of the following year marched north across the border. The two enemy forces met at Falkirk, where not only was Wallace deserted by his cavalry, but the English archers completely routed his pikemen, thereby ending the Scottish leader's ambitions for ever.

But 'Messire Williame le Waleys' himself had no intention of surrendering and managed to escape. For some months he carried on a guerrilla warfare but, achieving little and hoping to enlist help from allies on the Continent, he visited France and Italy. Despite all his efforts, no support was forthcoming from either Philip of France or Pope Boniface VIII and he returned to Scotland to resume his spasmodic attacks on the English forces occupying his country. By a dreadful irony however, his ultimate downfall was brought about, not by the 'enemy' but by erstwhile colleagues and fellow supporters, Red Comyn, Sir John Menteith (see p.146) and others, who cruelly betrayed him and on 4 August 1305 he was captured at Robroyston near Glasgow. He was held in the impregnable fortress of Dumbarton before being transported, heavily fettered and under strong guard, to London, arriving there on 22 August, when he was confined in a house owned by an alderman named William de Leyre.

The following day he was conveyed on horseback to Westminster Hall where, placed on a scaffold at one end of that building, he was made to wear a crown of laurels for having dared to boast to his followers that one day he would be crowned in the Hall of England's kings. He was accused of being a traitor and of sacrilege and robbery while conducting his guerrilla warfare; his defence, brief and logical, was that he could not be regarded as a traitor, for he had never sworn allegiance to the King. But this was brushed aside by the court and little time was wasted before he was sentenced to a traitor's death.

After the trial he was dragged through the streets of London tied to horses' tails, and on the next day was taken to Smithfield where he was hanged on gallows made especially high for the occasion, then taken down half-dead, disembowelled and quartered. His remains were exhibited on the city gates of Berwick, Stirling, Perth and Newcastle-on-Tyne, the quarter displayed at the latter city being accompanied by his amputated sword-hand.

In compliance with the official document promulgated at the time of his sentence, his head was mounted on a pike on London Bridge, 'in sight both of land and water travellers'. This was the first recorded instance of such a grisly deterrent being exposed there, and it was reported that the Londoners flocked in their thousands to view the dripping head of one whom they had been taught to believe was the devil incarnate, one who would have inflicted indescribable atrocities south of the Scottish border, had he not been caught and executed.

## WALTHEOF, EARL OF HUNTINGDON

There were beheadings by the sword prior to the Norman invasion of 1066, of course, but William the Conqueror introduced it into the judicial code as the extreme penalty for those of aristocratic blood, and Waltheof, one of the few surviving Saxon barons, was the first to be dispatched in that manner.

The son of Siward, Earl of Northumbria, a strong and powerful warrior adept with the battle-axe, he held the additional title of Earl of Northamptonshire, and must have accepted the occupation by the Normans with equanimity for in 1067 he accompanied the new King to Normandy, and although he took part when the Danes slaughtered the French garrison at York in 1069, he was pardoned by William in the following year. So highly was he thought of in court circles that shortly afterwards he married Judith, the King's niece, and was appointed Earl of Northumberland; riding high, no doubt the possibility of being accused of a crime of any nature, let alone suffering execution, would doubtless never have entered his mind. But he might have avoided such a death had he never met Judith, for it was rumoured that she tired of him and in fact, urged her uncle to rid her of his company, permanently. True or not, in 1075 he was arrested and charged with conspiring with the Danes in a plot to send an invasion fleet up the River Humber.

Waltheof was imprisoned at Winchester where he was tried and found guilty of high treason. One morning in 1076 he was awakened and told he was to be beheaded. Clad in his rich Earl's robes, he was escorted by soldiers and, together with a priest, conducted outside the walls of the ancient city. As the grim procession wended its way, Waltheof removed his chain of office, his medallions, brooches and other valuables, and gave them to those of the people who by then were hurrying alongside, curious to witness the rare event of a nobleman's execution.

The soldiers, uneasy at the increasing numbers of would-be spectators, coupled with a strong desire to get the unsavoury task over and done with – for the days of Tower Hill and Tyburn, when executions were welcomed by the masses as gratuitous entertainment, were far in the future – wasted little time in selecting the most appropriate spot, an area of rising ground not far from the walls. There, Waltheof lay down and commenced his prayers but, on being ordered to rise and bare his neck, he demurred, insisting that he should be allowed to continue and, kneeling, started to repeat the Lord's Prayer. By then a large crowd was starting to congregate, the people surging forward and jostling each other in order to see what was happening – for there was no scaffold to provide a clear view for everyone – and as more of the citizens streamed through the gates as the news spread, the soldiers realized that to avoid matters getting totally out of hand, no further time could be granted to the Earl. Accordingly, while Waltheof's lips still moved in prayer, one soldier stepped forward and, with one stroke of his sword, severed his head. While a priest completed the victim's abruptly interrupted prayer, the onlookers were forced to move back and, a hole being hastily dug in the ground, the head and body were rudely buried. Regarded as a popular hero and martyr, Waltheof, Saxon Earl of Huntingdon, was later buried in Crowland Abbey where his tomb is believed to have brought about many miracles.

## WARD, WILLIAM

This Roman Catholic gentleman was a secular priest, that is, one who became a priest in this country rather than being trained on the Continent. In 1641, a time when to be one of his calling was particularly perilous, he was arrested and although no charge was made against him, he was sentenced to be hanged, drawn and quartered at Tyburn.

At most such executions there were many of the same faith who endeavoured to acquire parts of the remains as holy relics, but this was strictly forbidden by the authorities who took rigorous measures to stop them, in most cases by surrounding the scaffold with the Sheriff's men and even soldiers. But there were always those who sought to defy the authorities by taking advantage of the confusion caused by the mêlée of people present, many among the crowd being hooligans who regularly attended executions solely in order to create mayhem by hurling not only oaths and abuse but also missiles, brickbats, rotten fruit and the like, at the officials on the scaffold and the executioner as he mutilated the victim. It was at such fraught moments that a determined Catholic would stake all on snatching whatever he could, a fragment of bone, a piece of bloodstained clothing or even some ashes from the fire in which the organs were being consumed by the flames. A high risk venture, for capture meant at best a prison sentence, at worst, a similar fate to the victim, a Catholic sympathizer caught in the very act.

But one small and very distinguished group of people who did manage to acquire such relics were some of the ambassadors of Catholic countries serving in England who, having diplomatic immunity, were not subject to the judicial power of the authorities. For instance, when Father Henry Morse was executed at Tyburn on 1 February 1645, the Portuguese Ambassador, Don Antonio de Sousa, and his French counterpart, the Marquis de Sabran, were present at the scaffold, both sending their footmen forward to dip their masters' handkerchiefs in the martyr's blood as holy souvenirs. But of all the ambassadors, none was more determined than the Spaniard who represented his country from 1640 to 1645, the Count Egmond, or to give him some of his imposing titles, Louis, Duke of Gueldres, Julliac and Cleves, Count of Ormund and Zutphen, Prince of Ghent, Count of Bures, Liège, etc.

The Count made it his business to attend as many executions of Catholics as possible, and during his term of office in England amassed an incredibly large collection of holy relics ranging from pieces of liver, viscera, fingers and leg bones, segments of burnt lung and lengths of windpipes to vertebrae, intestines and similar organs. Pieces of more material objects were not overlooked, the collection including ropes with which the victims were hanged, garments such as shirts worn by the doomed martyrs, the straw on which the victim had lain while being disembowelled and even the apron and sleeves belonging to the executioner. Those who vouched for the authenticity of these relics testified that 'we did recover by the assistance of our said domestics who, by our knowledge and command, and in our sight, and under the very eyes of the heretics, with no small risk of their lives, did snatch part of them out of the midst of the flames and the other parts did purchase of the executioner at the very time of the execution.'

His Excellency the Ambassador was unable to be present at the execution of the priest William Ward but Challoner, in his *Catholic Memoirs* published in 1843, described exactly what happened:

A person of great quality, Count Egmond by name, hearing by a servant of his who was present at the action, that an holy priest had suffered martyrdom that morning, asked him if he had brought any relic of the priest away with him, who told him Yes, and gave him the very handkerchief which the saint had cast out of his pocket. The Count, taking it with reverence, kissed it; but finding no blood upon the same, gave the servant his own handkerchief, commanding him to run back instantly to the place of execution, and to dip that in some of the martyr's blood, if he could find any.

The servant, posting away, came back to the gallows, made diligent search for some of the blood, but finding it was all scraped up by the zeal of other pious Catholics

221

who had been before him, takes his stick and, rubbing up
the ashes where the bowels of the martyr had been burnt,
finds a lump of flesh all parched and singed by the fiery
embers wherein it lay covered, and hastily wrapped up
what he had found, in the handkerchief which his lord
had given him, not having time to shake off the fiery coals
or hot ashes by reason that some malicious persons that
stood by, and saw this fellow stooping and taking somewhat out of the fire, demanded of him what he took
thence . . .

The account goes on to describe how the servant 'nimbly
slipped over a park pale [fence]' and ran for his life, hotly
pursued by the enemy, both on horse and foot. Resolved not to
lose the relic, he hastily dropped it, as he ran, into a bush,
taking care to mark its position so that he might return to find
it when the hue and cry was over. 'And this time he did drop it
with such dexterity, making no stop at all, but feigning a small
trip or stumble, and yet seeming to recover himself, ran on,
drawing his pursuers after him, to delude them, and thereby
save the relic. In brief this poor man recovered the outskirts of
the town ere he was overtaken.'

He was of course apprehended, but the ambassador's influence was to get him speedily released, and early next morning
he found the relic where he had left it in the park. It turned
out to be the martyr's heart, and it was considered miraculous
that the handkerchief that had enfolded it had not been burnt
nor singed by the hot embers which clung to it, while the heart
itself remained whole and seemingly unharmed for fifteen
days, when the Count had it embalmed 'not to preserve it from
corruption, which it seemed no way to incline to, but for reverence and religion to so rich a relic'.

The heart, together with the handkerchief William Ward
had in his hand when he died, his ring, probably taken from

his severed arm, and his diurnal, a service book containing all the canonical hours except matins, were also saved and doubtless are now items of veneration in a place of Catholic worship somewhere on the Continent.

# WILKINSON, JOHN
# MITCHEL, ANTHONY

These two robbers departed this life simply because they ignored the dreaded implications of the old saying quoted in the *Beggars and Vagrants Litany*, 'From Hell, Hull and Halifax, may God preserve us'. Hell, because of the inevitable purgatory, Hull because of the severity of its magistrates and bye-laws directed against vagrants – and Halifax because of the Gibbet. The duo paid dearly for their ignorance of that warning.

When apprehended they were placed in the stocks in the market place at Halifax 'both to strike terror into others and to produce new evidence against them'. Nearby was displayed their booty, sixteen yards of russet-coloured kersey, a thick woollen cloth, valued at one shilling a yard, six yards of cinnamon-coloured kersey and eight yards of white kersey 'frized for blankets', stolen from Samuel Colbeck, also two colts, one valued at three pounds, the other at forty-eight shillings.

Cloth-weaving was the local cottage industry, and the fact that, after being woven, the material was stretched out to dry over frames set up in neighbouring fields made the material an easy target for those of criminal intent. The frames themselves were known as 'tenters', the lengths of cloth being held taut by 'tenterhooks' – hence the popular saying applied to undue stress.

Wilkinson and Mitchel, each escorted by four men, were brought by the town bailiff to appear before a jury consisting of 'sixteen most ancient men', and after due deliberation of all the evidence presented by the prosecutors, the verdict of guilty was announced. As stated in the court records: 'Whereas by ancient custom and liberty of Halifax, the said John Wilkinson and Anthony Mitchel are to suffer death by having their heads severed and cut off from their bodies at the Halifax Gibbet. Unto which verdict we subscribe our names.'

They were returned to the market place, there to mount the high stone base, and in front of the multitude of spectators, each felon in turn confessed, then knelt, positioning his head between the two tall uprights, at the top of which was poised the heavily weighted blade. The rope tied to the retaining pin was stretched out into the crowd – those grasping it passed the more or less unanimous verdict – and on 30 April 1650, Wilkinson and Mitchel paid the price for their crimes, the last of the many, both men and women, who suffered beneath the Gibbet's falling blade.

# WYATT, SIR THOMAS

In 1553 the young and sickly Edward VI had died, having nominated Lady Jane Grey to succeed him, only for her to be displaced by Mary Tudor as the chosen queen. The political unrest was further exacerbated when Mary announced her intention to marry Philip of Spain, England's traditional enemy, and while some had already paid the price for their misplaced allegiance to Jane, others were determined to prevent the union at all costs. Sir Thomas Wyatt's efforts to stop the Queen's marriage cost him his head.

Sir Thomas, no stranger to military matters having served in France with distinction in the wars against Charles V, had settled down in his baronial residence, Allington Castle on the

River Medway in Kent, with his wife and their ten children, but not content with family life, hectic though it undoubtedly must have been, decided to take decisive action and lead a revolt against the Queen's intentions. Little did he realize that that would hasten, if not actually bring about the decapitation of Lady Jane Grey, then captive in the Tower.

In January 1554, his supporters being summoned by the ringing of the county's church bells, he recruited a force of ten thousand and, together with other influential Kentish knights and men of substance, he established his headquarters at Rochester, taking possession of its castle, then started a march towards London. As word spread of the impending attack on the city, a force led by the aged Duke of Norfolk intercepted them but, on hearing Wyatt pledge that they opposed not the Queen but the inevitable Spanish intrusion into English affairs, Norfolk's men switched sides, shouting, 'A Wyatt! A Wyatt!' Sir Thomas himself rode through their ranks, saying, 'So many as will come and tarry with us, shall be welcome, and as many as will depart, good leave have they.' Those who did depart were allowed to leave peaceably but on their return presented a sorry sight to the Londoners, their bows broken, their scabbards empty, their jackets turned inside out. With his army now considerably reinforced, Sir Thomas continued his advance, reaching Greenwich on 2 February, when 'that day the Lord Mayre's officers served him at dynner in harnis'.

Most historic battles fought in this country took place in comparatively isolated areas and open countryside, Marston Moor, Bosworth, Flodden Field and others, and so it is intriguing to realize that close combat, hand-to-hand fighting, actually took place in the localities and thoroughfares of London, the names of which are so familiar to most people. By 5 February Wyatt and his men were in Deptford – and the city was in a state of alarm, a city newspaper reporting:

This daie before noone all horsemen were by a drom [drum] commanded to be at sainct James felde and the footemen commanded to be ain Fynsbury felde to muster. This day, about iij [three] of the clocke, sir Thomas Wyat and the Kentyshemen marched forwarde from Debtford towardes London, being by estimation about ij thousand men; which their comying, so soone as it was perceyved, ther was shot off out oof the White tower a vii or viij shott; but myssed them, sometymes shoting over, and sometymes shoting short. After the knowledge thereof once had in London, forthwith the drawbridge [of London Bridge] was cutt downe and the bridge gates shut.

The inhabitants prepared themselves for the armed invasion: 'The mayre and the sheryves harnessyd theymselves and commanded eche man to shutt in their shoppes and wyndowes, and being redy in harnes to stande every one at his dore, what chance soever might happen.' The scene was one of panic, people running up and down the streets seeking refuge, weeping women and children, servants and maids fleeing into their houses, shutting and barring the doors.

By this time Wyatt, still south of the Thames, had got as far as Southwark; the local people did not oppose his men, indeed welcoming them with food and drink. Wyatt, a good military commander, saw that his men were paid and that they recompensed the locals for the fare; aware that a price had been put upon his head, he had the name 'Thomas Wyat' fixed on his cap in defiance. As the outpost of the Queen's troops had already withdrawn from the southern end of the bridge, he positioned two pieces of ordnance, cannon, there, and another opposite to the Tower, in Barmsey (Bermondsey) Street.

With a gap in the bridge where the drawbridge had been, a river crossing was out of the question; a reconnoitre had also established that the Tower's considerable fire power was being prepared, using the church towers of St Tooley's and St Maire Overies in Southwark as aiming points, Stow detailing the types of armament as 'seaven great pieces of ordnance, culverings and demi-canon, besides all the pieces on the White Tower, one culvering on the Diveling Tower and three fauconets over the Water Gate'. At that, Sir Thomas said, 'This place, Sirs, is too hot for us,' and, rather than have a neighbourhood so well disposed to him bombarded, he assembled his men and marched via Battersea, Wandsworth and Wimbledon to Kingston where, despite its bridge having been partially destroyed, he managed to cross the river by improvising a bridge of barges, and by way of Twickenham eventually reached Brentford, west of the capital, confident of receiving a welcome by the London citizens. He was to be bitterly disillusioned.

In the city, precautions were being taken by those surrounding the Queen, the chaplain of Whitehall's Royal Chapel wearing a coat of mail beneath his vestments while officiating at a Mass attended by Mary. After the service she returned to St James's and placed that palace in a state of siege, 3000 citizens volunteering to protect the area. On 7 February word came that Sir Thomas and 10,000 men were approaching Hyde Park Corner. The news caused havoc in the palace, barricades being erected in every corridor, guards stationed at every door and window, the Queen's ladies-in-waiting bewailing the fate of a sovereign whose very bedroom was filled with men in armour. Through it all Her Majesty remained calm and dignified, even when word came that the rear of Westminster Palace was under attack. The 500 infantrymen guarding that building were reinforced by more citizen volunteers, these even including some lawyers who, on their way to court, wore suits of armour under their legal robes. As the fierce fighting continued seemingly all over the city, at St James's the Queen's women, now in a paroxysm of terror, urged her to go by river and seek refuge in the Tower, but she refused and ordered them to retreat to the innermost part of the building.

Such was the rebels' momentum that they soon reached Charing Cross and, in scenes of wildest confusion, they forced their way along the Strand towards Ludgate. There not only was the Gate closed against them but they were also confronted by a body of troops led by the Captain-General, Lord William Howard. Had Wyatt been able to transport his heavy weapons across the makeshift bridge at Kingston, success could possibly have been achieved; as it was, despite some fierce hand-to-hand fighting, Wyatt and his men were driven back as far as Temple Bar, near Chancery Lane. There, while desperately attempting to regroup his forces, Wyatt was suddenly attacked by more royal troops under the command of Lord Clinton, a further and decisive blow being struck when Lord Pembroke's forces charged, their impetus scattering the opposition like chaff in the wind. Wyatt, realizing that his cause was lost, fled with some of his disorganized followers along Fleet Street. Here, 'his clothes torn, his face covered with blood, and all forlorn', he sought shelter in a fishmonger's stall opposite the 'Belle Sauvage' Inn at Ludgate. Too exhausted to resist further, his sword and dagger both gone, his armour smeared and dented, his velvet hat crushed in and filthy, he was taken prisoner by Sir Maurice Berkley and later escorted to the Tower, where he was greeted by the Lieutenant exclaiming, 'Oh thou Villain and traitor, if it was not that the law must pass upon thee, I would stick thee through with my dagger!'

Bereft of their leader, the demoralized rebels were soon rounded up and imprisoned, the gaols being so full that some had to be held in local churches. Awful retribution was subsequently meted out to them, more than four hundred being executed, many at Maidstone and Rochester in Kent. Fifty-eight were hanged on gallows erected at every gate of the city, one at the south end of London bridge, two at Leadenhall and others at Cheapside, Fleet Street, Smithfield, Holborn, Pepper Alley (Southwark), Bermondsey Street, Charing Cross, Hyde Park Corner and Tower Hill; fifty members of the trained bands (local militia) who had deserted to join Wyatt were captured and hanged without trial in front of their own shop and house doors, and the slaughter went on 'until the Queen could not go to the city without beholding the ugly sight of dangling corpses at every turn of the street.'

Sir Thomas was put on trial in Westminster Hall on 15 March and found guilty of high treason but the execution was postponed while attempts were made to make him incriminate Elizabeth, some reports alleging that he was racked. Whatever persuasion was administered, he absolved the Princess completely, and on Thursday 12 April he was taken to Tower Hill where 'after and by xj [eleven] of the cloke was he quartered on the skaffold and ys members burnt be-syd the skaffold. And so there was a care [cart] and a baskete, and the iiij quarters and hed was putt in-to a baskete to nuwgat to be parboyled.'

His quarters were displayed where it was considered they would be most effective, one at Pepper Alley, one above a city gate, another at Newington and the last quarter 'striking terror into the passers-by at St Thomas a Waterings in the Kent Road'. Instead of being piked on London Bridge, Sir Thomas's head was exhibited on the gibbet at Hay Hill, near Piccadilly, *Acts and Monuments of Martyrs* reporting, 'from whence it was stolne away, and great search made for the same.' Other sources state that the head was removed by friends and secretly buried.

And Queen Mary, while accepting the fact that her half-sister Elizabeth posed no immediate threat, was nevertheless fearful of further, perhaps even better equipped uprisings to replace her on the throne with yet another rival, and so reluctantly took the only step open to her – and ten days later Lady Jane Grey was beheaded.

# SELECT BIBLIOGRAPHY

Bayley, J. *Tower of London* (Caddell, 1825)

Bell, D. C. *Chapel in the Tower* (John Murray, 1877)

Camm, D. B. *Forgotten Shrines* (Macdonald and Evans, 1910)

Davey, R. *The Pageant of London* (Methuen, 1906)

Evelyn, J. *Diary of John Evelyn* (Bickers & Bush, 1879)

Hall, E. *Hall's Chronicles* (1809 edition)

Harman, A. *Sketch of the Tower of London* (Brook & Roberts, 1877)

Harrison, Yeoman Warder B. *Prisoners in the Tower*

Holinshed, R. *Holinshed's Chronicles* (edited Hooker, 1586)

Loftie, W. *Tower of London Authorised Guide* 1888

Mackay, J. *History of the Burgh of Canongate* (Anderson and Ferrier, 1900)

Marks, A. *Tyburn Tree, its History & Annals* (Brown, Langham, 1908)

Stow, J. *Survey of London* (Dent, 1912)

Tangye, Sir Richard *The Two Protectors, Oliver & Richard Cromwell* (Partridge, 1899)

Timbs, J. *Romance of London* (Warne, 1865)

Stanley, Dean A. P. *Memorials of Westminster Abbey* (Murray, 1911)

Sutherland-Gower, Lord Ronald *Tower of London* (Bell, 1901)

Thornbury, R. *Old and New London* (Cassell, Petter and Galpin 1893)

Williamson, A. *General Williamson's Diary* (Camden, 1912)
Williamson, M. G. *Edinburgh* (Methuen, 1906)

*Calendar of State Papers* (Domestic Series)
*Newgate Calendar & Criminal Recorder* (Miles & Co., 1891)
*Notable British Trials* series
*Tyburn Gallows* (London County Council, 1909)
*Tower of London Records*

# GENERAL INDEX

# Index

# Index of the One Hundred Selected Victims

HDQ = Hanged, Drawn and Quartered
HG = Halifax Gibbet
SM = Scottish Maiden